Apps for Learning, Middle School

iPad, iPod Touch, iPhone

21st Century Fluency Project

Andrew Churches

Andrew Churches is a teacher and ICT enthusiast. He teaches at Kristin School on Auckland's North Shore, a school with a mobile computing program that sees students with personal mobile devices and laptops. He is an edublogger, wiki author, and innovator. In 2008, Andrew's wiki, Educational Origami, was nominated for the Edublogs Best Wiki awards. He contributes to a number of web sites and blogs including Techlearning, *Spectrum Education* magazine, and the Committed Sardine blog. Andrew believes that to prepare our students for the future, we must prepare them for change and teach them to question, think, adapt, and modify.

Harry Dickens

Harry Dickens is the technology director for the Arkansas Public School Resource Center. Prior to his position at the center, Harry was a classroom teacher in Texarkana and El Dorado, Arkansas. He left the classroom to become the instructional technology director for the Texarkana School District. Harry teaches professional development classes on infusing technology into instruction throughout Arkansas, as well as at national conferences. He is a member of the core Technology Infused Education (TIE) team, a technology group of more than 100 instructional technology trainers in Arkansas. Harry is also a member of the Technology Information Center for Administrative Leadership (TICAL), which is a cadre of administrators that contributes new technology resources and provides orientation and training sessions throughout the state. He is currently serving on the Arkansas State technology planning committee and is chairing the teaching and learning subcommittee. Harry believes that receiving education content extends beyond district or state boundaries. He also believes we must embrace mobile technologies as a teaching tool, as well as a delivery mechanism for relevant content for classrooms. Harry and his wife, Quita, have two young sons, Harrison and Jordan.

21st Century Fluency Project

copublished with

CORWIN
A SAGE Company

For information:

21st Century Fluency Project Inc.
1890 Grant St.
Vancouver BC Canada V5L 2Y8

www.fluency21.com

ISBN-13: 978-1-4522-4306-1

Acquisitions Editor: Debra Stollenwerk
Design/Typesetting: Ross Crockett
Cover Design: Lee Crockett, Ross Crockett

Disclaimer: Every attempt has been made to contact known copyright holders included in this work. Any errors are unintended and should be brought to the attention of the publisher for corrections in subsequent printings.

SUSTAINABLE
FORESTRY
INITIATIVE

Certified Chain of Custody
Promoting Sustainable Forestry
www.sfiprogram.org
SFI-01268

SFI label applies to text stock

Contents

Introduction xi

Chapter 1—Tools for the Basics 1

Chapter 2—Tools for Literacy 13

Chapter 3—Tools for Social Studies 35

Chapter 4—Tools for Mathematics 47

Chapter 5—Tools for Science 61

Chapter 6—Tools for ESOL 79

Chapter 7—Tools for Speaking in Tongues 91

Chapter 8—Tools for Sharing and Talking 107

Chapter 9—Tools for Creating 127

Apps List 142

21st Century Fluency Project

The 21st Century Fluency Project is about moving vision into practice through the process of investigating the impact of technology on our society and our children over the last few decades, learning how we in education must evolve, and, finally, committing to changes at the classroom level.

Living on the Future Edge is the first book in our 21st Century Fluency Series. We face a world on the move, and education needs to react. A series of six books, as well as related supporting materials, has been developed in order to answer the following essential questions that teachers will ask when considering how educators and education must respond to the profound developments that are being experienced in the world at large.

Why Do I Have to Change?

Living on the Future Edge
Windows on Tomorrow

In this book, we discuss the power of paradigm to shape our thinking, the pressure that technological development is putting on our paradigm for teaching and learning, six exponential trends in technological development that we can't ignore, what these trends mean for education, new skills for students, new roles for teachers, and scenarios of education in the future.

Understanding the Digital Generation

Teaching and Learning in the New Digital Landscape

This book examines the effects that digital bombardment from constant exposure to electronic media has on kids in the new digital landscape and considers the profound implications this holds for the future of education. What does the latest neuroscientific and psychological research tell us about the role of intense and frequent experiences on the brain, particularly the young and impressionable brain?

Based on the research, what inferences can we make about kids' digital experiences and how these experiences are rewiring and reshaping their cognitive processes? More important, what are the implications for teaching, learning, and assessment in the new digital landscape?

How can we reconcile these new developments with current instructional practices, particularly in a climate of standards and accountability driven by high-stakes testing for all? What strategies can we use to appeal to the learning preferences and communication needs of digital learners while at the same time honoring our traditional assumptions and practices related to teaching, learning, and assessment?

Where Do I Start?

The Digital Diet

Today's Digital Tools in Small Bytes

This book offers bite-sized, progressively challenging projects to introduce the reader to the digital landscape of today. This is the world of our children and students. *The Digital Diet* will help readers shed pounds of assumptions and boost their digital metabolism to help keep pace with these kids by learning to use some simple yet powerful digital tools.

What Would This Teaching Look Like in My Classroom?

Literacy Is Not Enough

21st Century Fluencies for the Digital Age

It is no longer enough that we educate only to the standards of the traditional literacies. To be competent and capable in the 21st century requires a completely different set of skills—the 21st-century fluencies—that are identified and explained in detail in this book. The balance of the book introduces our framework for integrating these fluencies in our traditional curriculum.

21st Century Fluency Kits

These kits are subject- and grade-specific publications designed to integrate the teaching of 21st-century fluencies into today's curriculum and classroom. Included are detailed learning scenarios, resources, rubrics, and lesson plans with suggestions for high-tech, low-tech, or no-tech implementation. Also identified is the traditional content covered, as well as the standards and 21st-century fluencies each project covers.

Apps for Learning

Best iPad/iPod Touch/iPhone Apps

In the classroom of the 21st century, the power of mobility has begun to play a significant role in the learning experiences of our students. The ubiquitous digital devices they use so frequently and unconsciously can be harnessed as powerful tools for learning, creativity, and discovery. And, as the saying goes, "there's an app for that."

This remarkable and revealing three-book series on the best choices for learning apps in the classroom covers mobility apps categories for utilities, general classroom applications, and also specialty apps designed with unique learning tools that students can utilize both in class and on the go. Each book is devoted to a specific grade level—one each for elementary school, middle school, and high school.

The *Apps for Learning* books will show how both you and your students can get the most out of our versatile mobile technology and turn the classroom into a personal digital adventure in learning.

The 21st Century Fluency Project Web Site

www.fluency21.com

Our web site contains supplemental material that provides support for classroom teachers who are implementing 21st-century teaching. The site lets teachers access pre-made lesson plans that teach traditional content along with 21st-century fluencies. The site also provides teachers with a blank template for designing their own lessons for teaching 21st-century fluencies. In addition, there are other shared resources and a forum for additional collaboration and support.

How Can We Design Effective Schools for the 21st Century?

Teaching the Digital Generation

No More Cookie-Cutter High Schools

The world has changed. Young people have changed. But the same underlying assumptions about teachers, students, and instruction that have guided high school design for a hundred years continue to shape the way high schools are designed today. In fact, so much is assumed about the way a high school should look, that new schools are created from a long-established template without question. Strip away the skylights, the fancy foyers, and the high-tech PA systems, and new schools being constructed today look pretty much the way they did when most adults went to school.

This is a mismatch with reality. We need new designs that incorporate what we have learned about young people and how they learn best. This book outlines a new process for designing high schools and provides descriptions of several new models for how schools can be configured to better support learning.

Introduction

On January 22, 2011, Apple announced its 10 billionth application had been downloaded from the App Store. At that time, for the 160 million iPod Touch, iPhone, and iPad users worldwide, the App Store offered more than 400,000 apps, with 60,000 specifically developed for the iPad (*http://www.apple.com/pr/library/2011/01/22appstore.html*).

As of June 2012, there are more than 500,000 apps in the App Store. There have been more than 25 billion apps downloaded by users (*http://www.pcworld.com/article/251216/apple_reaches_25_billion_downloads_from_its_app_store.html*). The iPad, iPhone, and iPod Touch have revolutionized the concept of a media player, cell phone, and personal computing device, and it's not at all surprising that these devices have made their way into the classroom.

Initially treated with a degree of fear and skepticism, these tools have the potential to change the face of teaching and learning. No longer are they a single-purpose device like the early cellular or mobile phone, which allowed users to talk to or text a colleague. They are much more sophisticated than devices from a few short years ago that could only provide simple reminders and calendars, a camera, and a few games. The tools we have today are highly functional and powerful computers capable of not only consuming, but also creating.

Since the introduction of the first iPad, the camera quality has greatly improved. Speech Interpretation Recognition Interface (SIRI) is on all new iPhone 4s. The new iPad has audio dictation tools and a great retina display. The devices themselves are not all that has improved over their initial two years as tools, either. The apps have become tools for creating interactive books, cloud computing, digital learning, and more. iPads as 1:1 devices are becoming the change agent in many schools around the country.

This fall, Apple will release iOS 6 for the iPad 2, the new iPad, and the 4th generation iPod Touch, as well as the iPhone 3GS and the new iPhones. The update will give you more features to make the things you do every day even better. It will be free and easy to upgrade wirelessly on your iPhone, iPad, or iPod Touch the moment it's available. It features upgrades to maps and Siri for the new iPad, offline web browsing, and iCloud tabs. You can start browsing on one device and pick up where you left off on another. In addition, the iOS 6 guided access features will offer great assistive technology to help students with disabilities get the most out of their iPads. Autistic students, for example, can remain focused and on task. This will also be a major tool for teachers wanting to use the iPad to give assessments. Hopefully this will make taking online national assessments on an iPad happen in the near future!

Despite such phenomenal capabilities, some commentators have said devices such as the iPad are primarily for consumption in that they are designed to access and view or play media—and that may be the case for many users who have these devices at home. Even so, as a device for consumption, the "i" devices are media playing, communication and collaboration enabling, web surfing, and book reading tools with immense potential.

In a classroom setting, however, they move from a device for consumption to a device for production. While it is true that the ability to program and develop software on them is very limited, the application of programming in schools is usually limited to specialist subject areas. For the average student, this lack is insignificant since the "i" devices are overflowing with tools for creative expression, collaboration, and communication. Their portability, ease of use, and clean design make them appealing. Add to this their customization ability, the simplicity of adding further tools, and their potential for connectivity and accessibility, and it is easy to see why these devices are tools that can be used in the classroom, across the curriculum, and spanning all age ranges.

The diversity of applications available at low or no cost from the App Store allows users to develop documents, spreadsheets, and presentations; edit videos; create and record podcasts and music; create, edit, and manipulate graphics and images; produce mind maps, charts, comics, cartoons, and picture books; publish tweets, blogs, and wikis; surf the Internet; read and send emails; and audio conference one to one or one to many—and these are just a few of the creative and productive elements the devices are capable of.

From our experience with the range of students we teach and how our own children use these devices, we have seen even the youngest children—pre-kindergartners who are essentially illiterate—be able to navigate and manipulate the tools. The finger-driven interface is a natural extension for young and old—it's quick to learn, intuitive, and simple. One of the earliest motor skills to develop in children is the ability to point, and with this ability to point they are easily able to manipulate these devices.

As educators, we accept that the world our students graduate into is going to be a digital one. Let's face it, the world is experiencing exponential change, and clearly this means we must prepare students for the dynamically new environment they will face on graduation.

For most of our graduates, the last meaningful thing they will do with a pen is to write their last examination. We have witnessed first computers in labs, then computers in classrooms, and most recently laptop programs, with administrators and teachers recognizing that computers are not about just-in-case learning, but more about just-in-time capturing of the teachable moment. We have seen the change from these computer technologies being rare and expensive to what they are today—accessible, ubiquitous, and affordable. Our students bring powerful computers with Internet connectivity, real-time communication devices, cameras, audio recorders, media players, and productivity tools with them into the classroom.

The "i" devices are powerful, portable, affordable, and accessible—and they provide a real alternative to having class sets of computers, pods of laptops, and laboratories full of desktops. While these "traditional" tools still have a place in our schools, the "i" devices are a cost-efficient alternative.

Today, the world is our classroom. While most school administrators don't mind the pod of laptops moving between classes, they would be concerned with them moving beyond the boundaries of the buildings. And it is obviously impossible to take the computer lab into the field. However, "i" devices provide a solution for the use of technology beyond the confines of the four walls of our classrooms. Portable, robust, and connected, these devices open huge possibilities for education outside of school. The range of applications and ease of connection means that students can work in situ, making their learning experience immediate and, therefore, far more relevant.

What Is *Apps for Learning?*

Apps for Learning is a snapshot of some of the best and most appropriate applications for the iPad, iPod Touch, and iPhone for use in the classroom. Written by classroom practitioners for classroom practitioners, it ties together teaching experiences using these tools from across curriculum areas and throughout grade levels. The tools detailed in this book are ones with which we have had personal and professional experience, and they have been selected because of their practicality and applicability for use in the classroom.

For each app, we have given you the basics and the classroom application. The basics cover cost, application type, curriculum area (where applicable), and basic functions and features. The classroom application shows how we have applied the tool to our teaching and learning practice. Because of the limitations of space, these are detailed and specific to one or two examples, but in most cases, we have had many, many more applications for them in our classrooms. We have attempted to show a use for them that will spark you to apply these tools in your practice and to engage your creativity and passion for teaching to adapt these starters into a myriad of different forms and uses.

How to Use This Book

The best place to start is in the area you are passionate about. Whether it is language arts, mathematics, the sciences, media, or physical education, there are applications that will suit you. Read the description and classroom use, and install the application. Many of the tools we have suggested are free or are available in both low- or no-cost and premium forms.

We know the best way to learn anything about an application is to play with it. Be sure to investigate the different features of these apps and consider how you could use them personally, in your classroom, and beyond.

The apps selected are ones that can be used individually, as well as having application to class sets of devices. Whether it is Apple's iWorks Pages (for word processing), iThoughtsHD (a "mind mapping" tool), Adobe Photoshop PS Express (for enhancing your photos), or Comic Touch (a graphics application), these tools will enhance your teaching and your students' learning.

As with all things technology related, the world of apps is constantly changing. It's very important to remember that new and exciting apps with incredible learning potential are being created every day. Just as quickly, some apps are phasing out to make way for the new and improved. Please be aware that the apps profiled in the following pages are indicative of what was available at the time this book was printed. Although rare, you may find that one or two of the apps listed are no longer available. We strongly suggest that you keep a close eye on learning apps development to pinpoint others that may suit your needs above and beyond what this series offers. It's a big apps world out there, and it's waiting for you to go and explore it.

Have fun, play, and learn!

Chapter 1

Tools for
The Basics

1 Tools for the Basics

The middle school is a creative, dynamic, and exciting place for both teaching and learning. For the most part, it is free from the pressure and demands of the examinations that are a focus of high school. The middle years provide an opportunity to seize the teachable moment and to encourage and pursue creativity, while at the same time learning the skills and underlying knowledge that will lead to a successful high school career.

The middle years are quite varied in the demands and needs they present. To match these requirements, you must cater not only to the formal aspects of teaching and learning, but also to the creative aspects. The applications toolkit that the students and teachers have available to them has to be flexible, adaptable, and useful. The applications must also be useable by the wide range of ages that the middle school encompasses. There are, after all, leagues of difference between the young person entering the first middle school year and the young adult graduating to the lofty expectations of high school.

A lot happens in these formative years and we, as teachers of middle school students, are instrumental in shaping and nurturing their futures. Let's take a closer look at what is in a basic toolkit for the 21st-century middle school classroom.

The Toolkit

So what are the tools you can use in this dynamic and ever-changing learning environment? In the following chapters, we will discuss some of the uses of the tools in vignettes from the classrooms, but we need a basic toolkit to get started and begin the learning adventure.

The basic elements of the toolkit are:

- A productivity suite like Quickoffice or iWorks Numbers, Pages, and Keynote.

- A mind mapping tool like iThoughtsHD.

- An eBook reader like iBooks. iBooks allows the learner to access and view not only electronic books, but also PDF or "portable document format" files. Documents opened in iBooks are added to the PDF section of the Library (figure 1.1).

- A web browser like Safari; or if you need to use flash, then the Rover web browser would be more suitable. Rover is an application made expressly for education, and it includes content filtering.

Figure 1.1.—iBooks PDF shelf

These are the basic items, and many more will be outlined and placed in spotlights at each chapter's end. Some are free and others are by subscription. Also, this is not an exhaustive list, since at the time of the writing of this book there were more than 90,000 applications available specifically for the iPad.

The Core Applications

iWorks or Quickoffice

The start of any toolkit is the productivity suite of tools. The selection of which package you choose, Quickoffice or iWorks, will depend on a number of factors, but core to this should be compatibility with your other teaching and learning technologies. Should your school network and infrastructure be based around the Windows platform and suites of tools, then you may want to consider Quickoffice with its Microsoft file format compatibility as the best choice. Should your school have an Apple flavor, then the iWorks suite, which includes Numbers, Keynote, and Pages, may be better suited to your needs. There is no hard and fast rule—it is rather a decision each school must make based on its needs analysis.

The core applications are a word processor, a data processor, and a presentation tool. These are what we would use on a day-to-day basis for a huge range of classroom tasks and activities.

However, gone are the days of teaching a student to "do a PowerPoint," use a word processor, or make a spreadsheet. The use of these tools is deliberate and considered. In the initial stages, the teacher may direct and lead the use of the tools, but the intuitive nature of the tools means that many of the students will have quickly moved beyond the instructions and steps that the teacher has outlined.

Without guidance, our students—particularly the younger ones—will create documents and presentations that lack the clarity of purpose required. They will select fonts that are almost unreadable, use a rainbow of colors, and select a myriad of images to adorn their creations. They focus on the superficial aspects of presentation rather than the core learning outcomes. The teacher has to channel this creative drive to support learning while maintaining the *passion* for learning.

The 21st-century teacher develops a set of principles for the students. These are principles that can shift from application to application, whether it is iWorks Pages on the iPad, Microsoft Word on the laptop, or Google Documents in the cloud. They teach:

- *The Principles of Graphic Design*—This concerns how to lay out a document, whether it is a letter, report, essay, brochure, poster, email, or newsletter.

- *The Principles of Data Processing*—These are the skills and processes for collecting, collating, processing, and presenting data in suitable formats.

- *The Principles of Presentation*—These are the processes and skills required to present information.

The Principles of Graphic Design

Following principles does not limit creativity; rather, it channels it to creating documents and products that suit the purpose and audience. Applications like iWorks Pages and Quickoffice provide a blank canvas the students can fill.

The main principles that need to be considered when applying graphic design are:

- Is it suitable for the *audience?*
- Is it suitable for the *purpose?*
- Is it *readable?*
- Is it *balanced* in the use of whitespace, alignment, and images?
- Is it in *harmony* in its use of colors, text size, background, and so on?
- Is the document *consistent*, and is there *repetition* and *pattern?*

Brooke is a fifth-grade student who has researched and prepared a document on one of her favorite topics—cats. This is an interest topic that her teacher, Tracey, set for the class at the start of the school year in order to develop an understanding of her pupils. Brooke prepared the document in iWorks Pages (figure 1.2).

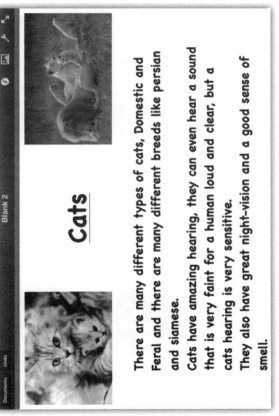

Figure 1.2—iBooks PDF shelf

Pages, like Quickoffice, allows her to lay out and format her document, choosing fonts and selecting colors, sizes, and alignment. She can easily add images, resizing and repositioning these to be either in line with text or to stand alone.

Tracey, her teacher, has instructed her in the basic principles of graphic design. When Brooke developed her document, she had to consider the audience and the purpose of the product. She considered her use of color and determined if her color selection made the text easier or more difficult to read. She chose serif or san serif fonts instead of scripting fonts because these are more readable. The images she added were suitable, not pixelated, and ethically sourced using a Google Images search that selected images available for reuse.

Principles of Data Processing

Lisa is a tenth-grade student who has been introduced to basic Mendelian genetics in her science class. The students look at various simple single allele traits such as attached earlobes, tongue rolling, and the "widow's peak"—the V-shaped growth of hair above the forehead.

These traits are controlled by a single gene and are simply identified. Lisa was asked to do a simple investigation to see how many students in her grade carried the double recessive trait for the widow's peak. To do this, Lisa created a spreadsheet in Numbers and she collected and collated two elements of information: the gender of the student, and the presence or absence of the widow's peak (figure 1.3). She used the camera on her smartphone to take example images of a widow's peak and a normal hairline.

Lisa stated in her hypothesis that she expected 25% of the population to have the widow's peak.

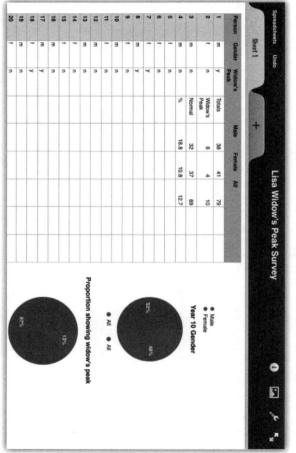

Figure 1.3—Spreadsheet in iWorks Numbers

Lisa collected the raw facts and figures and entered these into suitably titled columns. She then calculated the totals for each category and broke the categories down into component elements, presenting these in a table.

She decided that she could best represent the data using pie graphs and developed a series of charts. She added suitable titles, labels, and keys to each graph. Lisa did not use a line graph as the information was discontinuous—it was either "yes" or "no." A line graph would have been useful if she was collecting and processing continuous data. She considered using a bar chart, but felt that the pie graph better suited her needs.

Lisa collected, suitably collated, and processed the information into a form that was easy to access, read, and understand. The processing added value by transforming data, which is raw facts and figures, into information, which is processed data.

Nathaniel was collecting and processing information for a presentation he was giving to his sixth-grade science class. The students were investigating the solar system, and Nathaniel was using a mind map to collect, collate, and process his research. His presentation was called "Walking on Different Worlds." He identified the outcomes that he wanted for the presentation and then used the mind map to structure and answer some key questions. Using mind maps to collect and organize information is a key process in the knowledge acquisition process. Nathaniel used iThoughtsHD as his preferred mind mapping tool (figure 1.4).

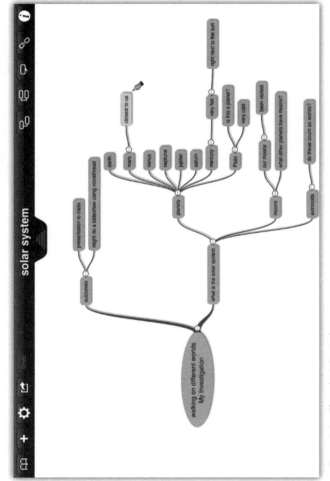

Figure 1.4—iThoughtsHD mind map

Brooke also used the iThoughtsHD app to organize information she needed for school assignments. In this task, she was researching two famous people she admired. She selected the two people who first conquered the world's highest peak—Mt. Everest, or Sagamatha, as the Nepalese people call it.

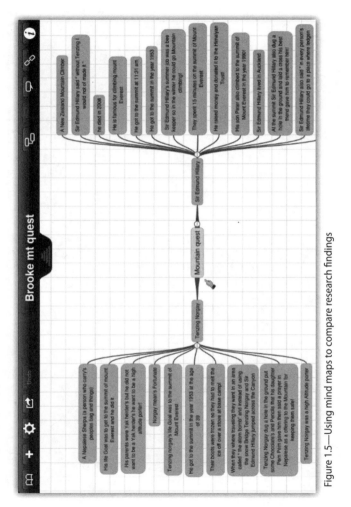

Figure 1.5—Using mind maps to compare research findings

Brooke collected information about Sir Edmund Hillary and Sherpa Tenzing Norgay, who together summited the peak of Mt. Everest in 1953 (figure 1.5). Brooke looked not only at the conquest, but also at the events and activities that each had been involved in since this historic achievement.

Mind maps or graphical organizers can be used to structure and organize information, making it easy to see and consider. This example (figure 1.6) is a simple "compare and contrast" template in iThoughtsHD, which a student could use to compare a topic or question, detailing the positive and negative aspects of the topic, and then summarizing their deliberations in the summary.

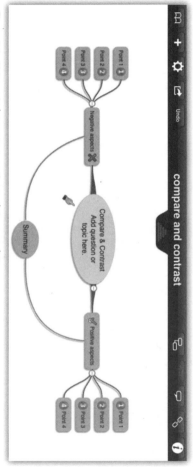

Figure 1.6—Using mind maps to organize and strucure data

Principles of Presentation

Nathaniel's presentation, "Walking on Different Worlds," looked at the different planets within our solar system. He used the mind map to structure and lay out his presentation, and then built the slideshow from this plan in Keynote (figure 1.7).

Figure 1.7—Student presentation in iWorks Keynote

He choose a black background as this matched the blackness of space. The images he selected also had a black background to match the background of the slides.

Nathaniel added detailed notes to the presenter's slides to avoid putting large amounts of text on the slides. Instead, he added a few keywords to talk about, rather than using large sentences that distracted from the audience's attention to his speech. He made sure the text was large, using at least a 28-point font to make it easily readable by his audience. He was also careful and consistent in his use of color with his text and background to enhance the readability of the slides.

The images he selected were carefully considered before being added to the presentation. Each of the images related clearly to the topic he was discussing at the time. The images were large, so they were not pixellated or distorted. Nathaniel used the Mask option to remove the borders from some of the images.

Nathaniel considered the following core questions when he developed his presentation: What is the purpose of the presentation, and who is the audience? He considered readability, consistency, pattern, and repetition. He avoided the common mistake of adding vast amounts of text to each slide, keeping to keywords and speaking about each of these. The smallest size text he used was 28 points, so it was easily readable. Nathaniel prepared presenter's notes that were then displayed on his iPad screen when the presentation was projected through the projector onto the screen. This gave him his script for his speech.

So for review, let's recap the main principles for proper presentation development that Nathaniel considered in his project:

• Keep words to a minimum.

• Be consistent in use of color, themes, and layouts.

• Ensure images are suitable, not pixelated, and relate to the topic.

• Have a logical flow in the arrangement of slides.

• Never have a font smaller than 28 points, and avoid scripting or decorative fonts.

• No more than seven words in a sentence and no more than seven points to a page.

Working with Images

There are a range of tools that are available on the iPad that will allow the user to capture and/or manipulate images. Some are free tools like Adobe Photoshop Express, while others such as Apple's iPhoto and Adobe's Photoshop Touch offer an extensive package of tools to suit all but the most demanding of users.

The iPad's photos container has some basic image editing functions built in (figure 1.8):

• Rotate

• Enhance

• Red eye removal

• Crop

Figure 1.8—Image editing options in photo container

A more flexible tool is Adobe Photoshop Express. This is a free application with add-ons available for purchase. Photoshop Express adds considerably more flexibility and a wider, more powerful tool set that the learners can use to manipulate their images. These tools include:

- *Crop tools*—including Crop, Straighten, Rotate, and Flip

- *Color tools*—including Exposure, Saturation, Tint, Black and White, and Contrast (figure 1.9)

- *Focus tools*—Sketch, Soft Focus, Sharpen, and Reduce Noise

- *Effects and Border tools*

With both the iPad 2 and the new iPad, pictures can be easily captured using the two cameras built into the device. The camera on the back of the iPad has the best resolution and quality. It is simple to switch between the two cameras by toggling the camera button in the bottom right-hand corner of the camera window (figure 1.10).

Figure 1.9—Adobe Photoshop Express image tools

Figure 1.10—Camera toggle button (bottom right-hand corner)

The camera window has four controls: the picture button to take the shot, the camera toggle button to switch between the front and rear cameras, the slider to switch between capturing still pictures and video footage, and the options button that allows you to switch the grid on or off.

As part of the research for his assignment, Nathaniel used his telescope at home to make observations of the night sky. He used the iPad's camera to take a picture of the telescope so he could include it in his presentation.

He switched on the grid in the options menu so he could get a balanced picture, using the grid lines to frame up the main picture element (figure 1.11). Selecting the rear camera also gave him the best quality in the image he took. He took several shots and compared each in the photos container to find the shot he felt best suited his purpose. He deleted the other shots to manage the available space on his iPad.

Figure 1.11—Image grid display

Adobe's Photoshop Touch and Apple's iPhoto add a number of extra tools and features that will fulfill the needs of most students (figure 1.12). Apple's iPhoto, a recent addition to the iWorks tool kit, links to the photos container and the camera roll and provides an organizational tool set as well as the obvious image editing features. iPhoto allows the user to adjust and manipulate the image by:

- Cropping and straightening

- Adjusting exposure

- Adjusting color

- Applying brushes to repair, remove red eye, saturate, desaturate, and lighten or darken the image

- Applying various effects including artistic, vintage, aura, black and white, and more

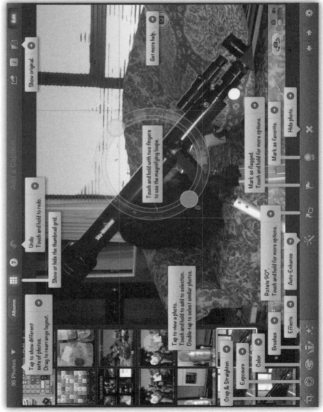

Figure 1.12—The tool/options range for photo editing

In summary, the iPad allows students to complete almost all of their day-to-day learning tasks. However, there is still a need for building a basic toolkit or suite of applications to meet these minimum needs or requirements.

The Basics—A Toolkit Summary

Product	Free or Purchase	Best Classroom Activity
iWorks Pages	Purchase	Processing text into documents like reports, brochures, simple word processing, and desktop publishing
Quickoffice HD	Purchase	
iWorks Keynote	Purchase	Presenting information in a slideshow format
Quickoffice HD	Purchase	
iWorks Numbers	Purchase	Processing and organizing data into tables and charts
Quickoffice HD	Purchase	
iThoughtsHD	Purchase	Organizing information into mind maps and graphical organizers
Popplet	Free/purchase versions	
SimpleMind+	Free/purchase versions	
iBooks	Free	
Kindle	Free	
Adobe Reader (PDF)	Free	EBook or PDF reader
Photos	Installed	Image editor—Basic
Adobe Photoshop Express	Free	
iWorks iPhoto	Purchase	Image Editor—Advanced
Adobe Photoshop Touch	Purchase	
Safari	Installed	Web browser
Rover (Flash enabled)	Free	

Chapter 2

Tools for Literacy

2 Tools for Literacy

This chapter explores how applications are used to enhance the Common Core State Standards (CCSS) for English language arts. The applications and scenarios are infused with 21st-century skills as well. The apps selected cover defining words, grammar, storytelling, cross-curricular activities, reading fluency, spelling, spoken and written language, building grammatically correct sentences, and presenting topics coherently. This chapter primarily focuses on English language arts but expands to cover other content areas. The applications selected and detailed here are Grammar Express: Parts of Speech, Tenses, Active and Passive Voice, and Nouns HD; iLive Grammar Botany, Autumn, and Winter; Spelling Test; SpellBoard and SpellBoard Buddy; StoryKit; Puppet Pals HD; Dictionary; Drawing Pad; iBooks, Book Creator, and Young Reader.

Grammar Express Apps

As students move into higher grades, they are required to use more sophisticated writing and speaking practices. Jordan is a middle school student who has to demonstrate how well he understands the conventions of standard English grammar and usage when writing or speaking. The Grammar Express apps for Parts of Speech, Tenses, Nouns, and Active and Passive Voice can help him understand, recognize, and correct inappropriate shifts in verb tense. He will also understand perfect verb tenses and much more. These skills are needed to be an effective 21st-century collaborator, communicator, and creator. When students are interacting with people from all over the world using various communication tools, using correct parts of speech and proper grammar are important. When creating stories, proficient grammar skills are needed for creating audio or text for storytelling activities.

Grammar Express: Parts of Speech contains more than 130 pages of grammar lessons. The app also contains more than 1,000 examples with grammar rules, and there are also test questions with explanations. Custom timer settings can help improve response times under challenging exam constraints. Grammar Express: Parts of Speech can help Jordan master usage of the eight different parts of speech.

The lessons on each page offer detailed explanations of each part of speech with several examples (figure 2.1). Jordan can learn the grammar rules, study the examples, and then test his understanding by taking quizzes.

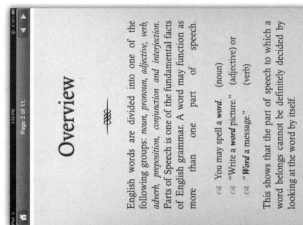

Figure 2.1—Grammar Express lesson overview

At the end of each quiz, he is presented with a test summary and an explanation for each test question (figure 2.2).

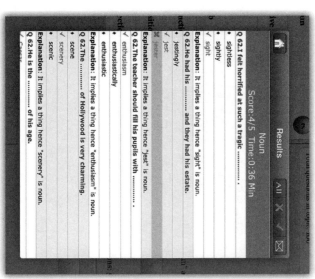

Figure 2.2—Grammar Express test summary

This app is great for individual use, but with the iPad 2 connected to a projector or compatible television with either an Apple VGA or digital AV adapter, teachers can use the Grammar Express apps for whole-group teaching. Teachers are tapping into Information Fluency by presenting the content visually so all students in the classroom can see what a correct or incorrect sentence looks like using their iPads.

The other Grammar Express apps work in a similar fashion as the Parts of Speech app. Grammar Express: Tenses contains more than 100 pages of lessons explaining each grammar tense with several examples. Jordan can learn the grammar rules, study the examples, and then test himself at anytime for understanding by taking quizzes.

Grammar Express: Active and Passive Voice helps with the transformation of sentences, a process which enables you to change a sentence from one grammatical form to another without changing its meaning. It contains more than forty-six pages of lessons with several examples explaining how to change active voice into passive voice, and vice versa.

When Jordan needs assistance with nouns and relative pronouns, the Grammar Express: Nouns HD app will help him master the different kinds of nouns such as common nouns, proper nouns, collective nouns, material nouns, and abstract nouns. It contains more than forty-eight pages of lessons explaining noun-number, gender, and case with several examples.

The Grammar Express quizzes can range from five to one hundred questions. Once quizzes are taken with any of the Grammar Express apps, the results can be emailed to parents or teachers. An explanation of how the answers are correct is in the end of the quiz results.

What Happened? (Grammar Express Apps)

The students will understand that tenses and voice, when used correctly, are very important when explaining something to others. The Grammar Express apps help build a foundation in language, which is important for students in gaining control over many conventions of standard English grammar, usage, and mechanics. Also, it helps them to learn other ways to use language to convey meaning effectively. Using these apps, the students will easily learn to demonstrate command of the conventions of standard English grammar and usage when writing or speaking. In the Grammar Express: Parts of Speech app, students learn to identify and correctly use patterns of word changes that indicate different meanings or parts of speech (e.g., presidential, preside, president).

iLiveGrammar: Autumn, Botany, and Winter

Sentences are more than just scientific facts, but also a means for introducing grammar. All three iLiveGrammar apps are supplemental teaching tools for the language arts and science curriculums. The apps cover different aspects of the fall and winter seasons and botany, but the hope is that this app will spark Jordan's interest and conversations about science. With iLiveGrammar Autumn, he can watch videos describing Earth science, animal behavior, and other fun topics, accompanied with beautiful photographs. The iLiveGrammar Winter app lets him see visual samples of the winter-related wildlife, as well as snowflakes and glaciers. The iLiveGrammar Botany app videos have everything from plants and their flowers and seeds, to leaf sizes and shapes (figure 2.3). These videos can be spaced so a new video shows after a set number of correct responses are given, ranging between one, five, ten, fifteen, and twenty correct responses.

There are four lessons:

- *Lesson 1:* Nouns and Verbs

- *Lesson 2:* Adjectives and Adverbs

- *Lesson 3:* Prepositions, Articles, Nouns, and Conjunctions

- *Lesson 4:* Review

Figure 2.3—iLiveGrammar Botany video

The apps randomly generate the sentences and photographs using a combination of words appropriate to the theme, so that each test is different. The sentences are associated with pictures with specific words or highlighted words (figure 2.4).

Figure 2.4—iLive Grammar Botany random sentence with highlight

The app also has a mirroring option that allows for these apps to display not just on the iPad 2, but on the first generation iPad as well. The Teacher screen displays the correct answers to all the questions.

Sample Questions from iLiveGrammar

Autumn

"The ground squirrel disperses **seeds**."—The highlighted word "seeds" is a noun. A noun is the name of a person, place, thing, or idea.

Correct answer: *noun*

Winter

"In the northern hemisphere, from the frigid **months** of December to February, I sighted polar bears."—The highlighted word "months" is a noun. A noun is the name of a person, place, thing, or idea. In this sentence, it is the object of the prepositional phrase.

Correct answer: *noun*

Botany

"The wind **amazingly** spreads tiny seedpods."—The highlighted word "amazingly" is an adverb. An adverb modifies an adjective, verb, or other adverb expressing a relation of place, time, circumstance, etc.

Correct answer: *adverb*

What Happened? (iLiveGrammar)

Besides being great for review and reinforcement, the iLiveGrammar applications offer cross-curricular activities, and vocabulary expansion happens as students actually work through the activities. The videos are also curiosity builders, especially when they are spaced throughout the activities. The videos are visual links to the question as well as the picture on the screen. The links to Wikipedia content are also a plus for the curious student.

Spelling Test

Jordan can create his own practice spelling test with the Spelling Test App. He practices the same words he gets in homework. With My Spelling Test, Jordan creates the test and decides which words to add (figure 2.5). After each test, his scores and which words were misspelled are saved and can even be emailed to parents or teachers (figure 2.6). My Spelling Test was designed so that students could make tests and practice on their own. It's a breeze for them to add words, take tests, and see their scores. After installing My Spelling Test on his iPhone or iPod Touch, Jordan can practice his spelling anytime, anywhere. He can practice while he is riding in the car or on the bus, waiting in line someplace, or just being at home.

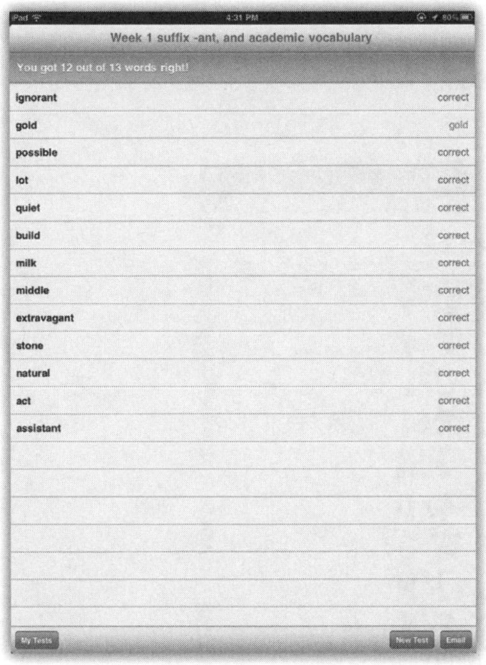

Figure 2.5—A typical test in the Spelling Test app

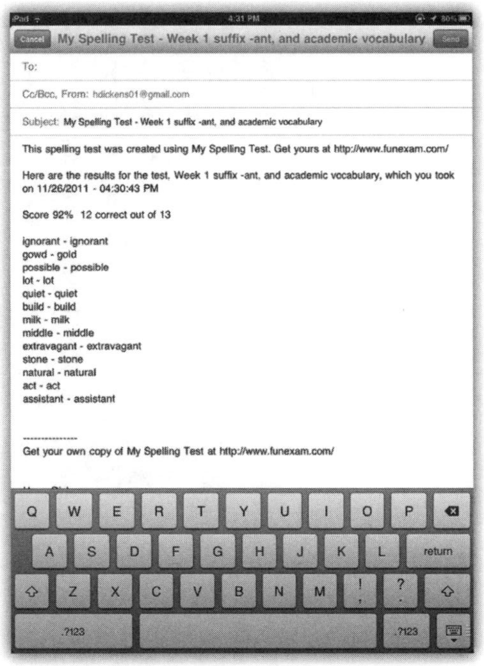

Figure 2.6—Test results ready to be emailed

SpellBoard

With SpellBoard, Jordan can study quizzes with the help of audio annunciation of the words and audio/text sentences using the words. There is also a dictionary in the app's study mode. Teachers can create spelling tests in the app for students who have missed a test. Synonym clues can be added to the quiz so that Jordan can eliminate the words that sound similar to the word he is spelling. Antonym clues could be used if teachers were to create an assessment on opposites.

This app can be used in a foreign language, social studies, science, and other classroom practice using words in a sentence or a spelling list. Extensions of this activity could be students creating the most interesting sentence with the SpellBoard or app. These sentences could be shared by connecting iPad or iPod Touch devices to an Apple TV with speakers.

SpellBoard Buddy

SpellBoard Buddy is the companion app for SpellBoard. It works on the iPad, iPod Touch, and iPhone. Quizzes can be loaded from iTunes or via Bluetooth. Once a quiz is done, the student's score is recorded and he or she can review any missed words. If there are a limited number of devices, the app will allow for the creation of a different account for each student. The latest update to SpellBoard and SpellBoard Buddy includes a word search activity from spelling lists (figure 2.7).

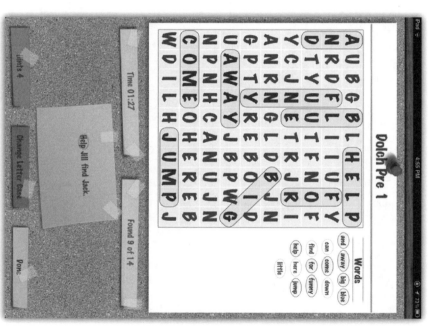

Figure 2.7—SpellBoard Buddy word search

What Happened? (Spelling Apps)

These apps allow teachers and students to create their own content in a 1:1 situation. These spelling test apps can be used in other courses to deepen understanding of the content. In the science or social studies classrooms, students could create sentences that use the important words to remember. Students are not only remembering the words, but also can be challenged to create complex sentences to share with classmates before and after spelling tests.

Presentation of Knowledge and Ideas

Jordan needs an activity that will help clarify the meaning of unknown words. Using Puppet Pals HD or StoryKit, he can create graphics to match the words he is creating for the activity. Students can add multimedia to aid in comprehension. The following apps cover the Common Core State Standards that state students should integrate multimedia and visual displays into presentations to clarify information, strengthen claims and evidence, and add interest. Since there is audio available in both Puppet Pals HD and StoryKit, students can demonstrate command of formal English. Puppet Pals allows the user to create multimedia projects with audio and still images (figure 2.8). There can be up to eight characters and five different backgrounds per project. Using Puppet Pals HD or StoryKit, the student's artistic proficiency will make use of creativity fluency by adding meaning to the storytelling. A student's imagination can really come to life with these applications.

Figure 2.8—Puppet Pals HD

StoryKit

Using StoryKit in middle school language arts is a great choice, both for the writing process and also the presentation of knowledge and ideas. Jordan creates a writer's notebook using StoryKit. Using audio, text, and images, he can write about such topics as:

- A particular tradition in his family

- An artifact like an arrowhead, ring, or antique—important objects in a student's life often provide excellent material to write about (figure 2.9)

- A special place like a certain room, attic nook, inside of a tree, or a scary closet— he might start by quickly sketching a map of a house full of memories

- A brother, sister, or special relative— he can focus on one aspect of that person or one experience he had with him or her

- His place in the family—oldest, youngest, middle child, only child adopted

- His best friend

- Moving—did he leave behind a best friend when moving from his old house

The list can go on and on. . . .

In the edit mode of StoryKit, Jordan can resequence his pages to develop the storyline to hook his readers. StoryKit is a great way to use an available technology like the iPad or iPod Touch to publish to an audience of peers, parents, and teachers.

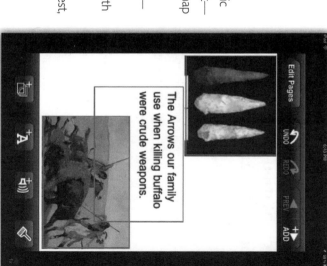

Figure 2.9—StoryKit examines arrowheads

Puppet Pals HD

Puppet Pals HD offers an easy way for Jordan to create and record his own animated shorts. The app only comes with one set of eight Wild West characters (two of which are a horse and a tumbleweed). However, there are twelve other character sets available for purchase at 99¢ each or $2.99 for all character sets, plus the option to use the camera inside the app. Character sets include categories such as politicians, holidays, entertainers, fairy tale characters, animals, and many more. A version called Puppet Pals for iPhone is also available.

The app's most appealing feature is its ability to cut people out of your real-life photos or images collected from the Internet and use them as puppets. Jordan can simply choose his characters and a background, resize the images, and when he's ready, he can push the Record button, move the characters around, and narrate his story. The app's educational value is limitless (literacy, listening and speaking, and drama). Using the PuppetPals HD app, Jordan can gather relevant information from multiple digital sources and assess the credibility and accuracy of each source.

Literacy in Writing, History/Social Studies, Science, and Technical Subjects Standards (WHST) are integrated into his writing. The project he creates could show his understanding of the forms and roles of government (figure 2.10).

Figure 2.10—Politics with Puppet Pals HD

Examples for social studies standards are identifying elected officials (eg., terms and qualifications) or creation of a presentation that shows Jordan's understanding of political parties and movements. The app can also be used to identify the purpose of the founding documents. Activities here show students creating digital products that reflect their understanding of content, which is a good demonstration of media fluency.

What Happened? (Storytelling Apps)

Sharing what students know about a topic is a great way to use the storytelling applications. Students can create personal narratives about themselves, or they can use the apps as interview tools. Still shots can be captured and audio tracks can be added to either a page in StoryKit or a background setting in Puppet Pals HD. With the eight characters in Puppet Pals HD, the roles can be divided and several students can collaborate on one project.

Dictionary

If there is a word that Jordan doesn't quite know the meaning of, the Dictionary app can help. It contains more than two million words, and it can even be used offline. The Dictionary app assists students both with the pronunciation of words and also how to use them properly in different parts of speech (figure 2.11).

For example, the word "color" is a noun when describing the natural appearance of the skin. The word can also be a verb when someone is coloring in a coloring book. The Dictionary app can be useful in helping to explain the meaning of common idioms as well as synonyms and antonyms.

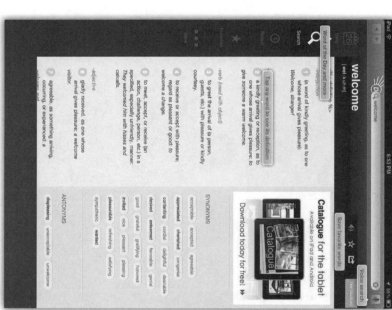

Figure 2.11—The Dictionary app

Drawing Pad

Jordan's assignment is to give the meaning of *personification* and write sentences with the object being personified. He loves drawing and would like to illustrate the sentences, rather than writing short answers. Jordan can create his own art using "actual-sized" photo-realistic crayons, markers, paintbrushes, colored pencils, stickers, roller pens, and more. Jordan can even save his artwork to his Drawing Pad album and reload it later to keep working on a masterpiece. After completing the drawing, it can be saved to iPhoto, the iPhone or iPad camera roll, shared via email, Twitter, or Facebook; or sent to a printer. The Blender tool allows you to soften and blend colors. Additionally, photo stickers are included (for the not-so-artistic!). One finger can be used to move the photo, and two fingers are used to rotate and resize it. Anyone can be creative with the variety of colors and textures available in this art app.

Drawing Pad supports the iPad's multi-touch screen and allows users to pinch and adjust the size of the stickers. Users also have the option of locking the stickers in place or moving them forward or backward in a drawing. Any of the sentences on the following page can be turned into a drawing.

- The wind sang her mournful song through the falling leaves.

- The microwave timer told me it was time to turn my TV dinner.

- The video camera observed the whole scene.

- The strawberries seemed to sing, "Eat me first!" (figure 2.12)

- The rain kissed my cheeks as it fell.

- The daffodils nodded their yellow heads at the walkers.

- The water beckoned invitingly to the hot swimmers.

- The snow whispered as it fell to the ground during the early morning hours.

- The china danced on the shelves during the earthquake.

- The car engine coughed and sputtered when it started during the blizzard.

Figure 2.12—The strawberries seemed to sing, "Eat me first!"

iBooks

With iBooks, students and teachers have a beautiful bookshelf of books, ePub, ibooks, and PDFs for their reading experience. The iBooks app has a convenient way to browse, sample, and buy books. Simply download the free iBooks app from the App Store and buy everything from classics and best sellers to enhanced books from the built-in iBookstore. Once you've downloaded a book, it appears on your bookshelf. Just tap it to start reading.

A new addition to the iBooks platform called iBooks Author allows the user to create interactive books. The app also reads the .epub and .ibooks format from documents created with Pages (.epub) or the iBooks Author app (.ibooks) from a Mac computer. Now students and teachers can create ebooks with audio, video, and weblinks (figures 2.13 and 2.14).

PDF	Word	RTF	Plain Text	ePub

Create an ePub document that can be read in iBooks.

Note that not all Pages formatting options are available in ePub. Learn more about ePub.

Title
Hope School District iPad Training

Author
Harry Dickens

Genre

☑ Use first page as book cover image

Cancel   Next...

Fig 2.13—Exporting to ePub options

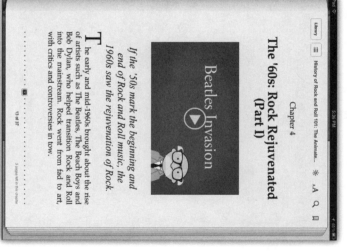

Figure 2.14—Video embedded in an ebook page

Students as well as teachers can create interactive books with multimedia, assessment questions, calculators, and even 3-D objects with iBooks Author (figures 2.15 and 2.16).

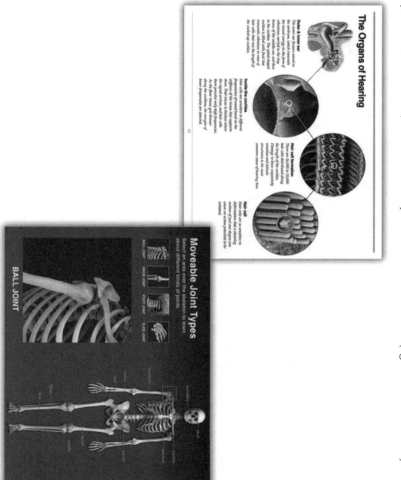

Figures 2.15 and 2.16—Screenshots of the ebook Life on Earth by Edward O. Wilson.
(source: http://itunes.apple.com)

Books can be added to iBooks through the App Store in iTunes or from education websites. Students and teachers can browse the table of contents of a book (figure 2.17), adjust the brightness of the book, and change the font size and style. Jordan can search with the Spotlight feature while reading a book.

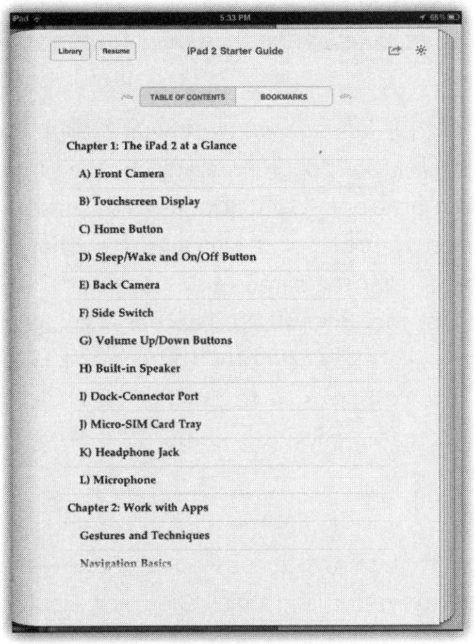

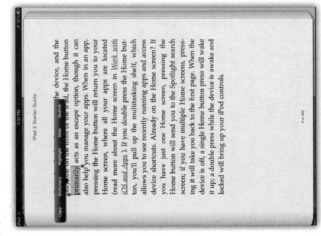

Figure 2.17—iBook table of contents

He can create bookmarks where he left off in reading. When a word is highlighted in an ebook, Jordan can copy text for another application, look up a word in the dictionary, highlight text, add a note to the document, or search for the word in other sections of the book and in Google or Wikipedia (figure 2.18).

Figure 2.18—Highlighting text in an ebook

With iBooks, there are limitless opportunities for students and teachers to import PDF documents into iBooks. From a connected computer, students or teachers could drag and drop PDF documents into the iTunes library, from a shared Dropbox or Box.net folder on a Mac or PC, or download them from an email attachment. Jordan can create ebooks on PCs using Open Office with an ebooks plugin or MS Word documents. They can be uploaded to sites like www.2epub.com and then downloaded to the iPad, iPod Touch, or iPhone as ePub documents.

Book Creator

Book Creator offers users something previously unavailable—the chance to create books on the iPad, which can be submitted and then read using Apple's iBooks.

Anyone who has worked with basic photo editing software will be comfortable with Book Creator. This app allows the user to add photos and text and change the background color on each page of the book (the developers also say in the iTunes description that future upgrades will include the ability to add video). Users can begin by taking the app's tutorial, which is cleverly designed as a book. This introduction to Book Creator allows the user to edit within the tutorial itself, so it's easy to become familiar with the application's interface.

Jordan can now create ebooks directly on the iPad. There is no need to create books with authoring tools that may be very complicated to use. After recent updates, the ability to add audio books is a major plus with this application. The app now allows students to create their own audio for books as well as importing files from their iTunes library.

The app also has a feature called Sound Track that can be played when a person begins to read the book in iBooks. This sound track could be played on one page or set to play throughout the book. The user adds text by selecting the box marked with the upper and lowercase "T" in the upper right-hand corner of the screen. After text is added, the font, text size, and color of the text can be changed. The background color can be changed in a similar manner. The app remembers both the last text setting and the last several colors used, which is helpful for maintaining uniformity throughout the book. Images can be inserted from the camera roll of the iPad.

To view the created book in iBooks is simple: Choose "Open in iBooks" from the menu in the upper left. It looks just like other ebooks on the bookshelf!

After creating an ebook, Jordan can simply drag and drop it into the iTunes library. Using this feature, he can create a documentary and have primary document audio and video resources inside his book. Using iBooks in this fashion is a great way for students to build collaborative projects as well as share what they know about a topic in a digital way. Users have the same ebook options they would have with an ebook downloaded from the iBookstore. Teachers can create ebooks using the ePub or iBooks format to create lesson notes and provide links inside the ebook to assessments created in Google Forms or to practice items inside the ebook. iBooks is great for class handouts, research papers, and more.

What Happened? (Book Creation and Reading from the iPad)

The updated iBooks and the new iBooks Author applications can be a classroom teacher's way to organize more and print less. One of the middle school standards requires students to include multimedia components and visual displays in presentations to clarify information. With iBooks Author, students can create books as well as add interactive widgets in the books they create. By using the multimedia features that are available in iBooks Author, books can be an interactive part of the class.

As teachers begin to get familiar with this authoring tool, they can then facilitate student use of the tool to create reports and projects that are interactive. Students can even create study cards from teacher-created iBooks. Content that is both relevant and interactive is something that will excite students. Away goes the book report, and it moves to students creating their own books that actually report themselves! Solution Fluency—the 6D process of Define, Discover, Dream, Design, Deliver, and Debrief—can be achieved by creating interactive digital books for iBooks.

Craft and Structure and Integration of Knowledge and Ideas

Young Reader

Rigor is infused throughout the Common Core State Standards. The requirements are for students to read increasingly complete text. Young Reader is the QuickReader edition for children, and it features thousands of classic children's books for free. Books by authors such as Coelho, Twain, Dickens, Kipling, Wilde, and London are available in the catalog (figure 2.19).

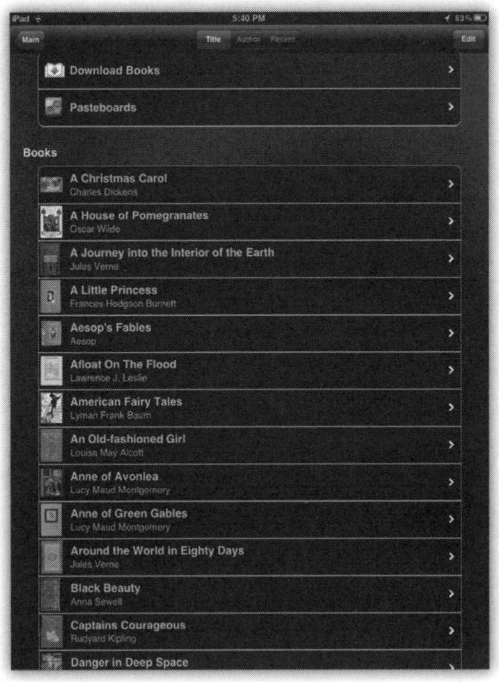

Figure 2.19—Young Reader book list

Additional books can be loaded from online catalogs. QuickReader features a highly elegant and customizable interface and includes normal reading and speed reading modes. The Young Reader app is targeted at children ages 8–13 and is designed to improve their reading skills. The app has more than 130 age-appropriate classic children's books preloaded in its content.

Jordan can explain how an author develops the point of view of the narrator or speaker in a text. Common Core State Standards (CCSS) ask students to compare and contrast the experience of reading a story, drama, or poem to listening to an audio file, viewing a video, or seeing a live interpretation of the text. CCSS also require students to compare and contrast texts in different forms (e.g., stories, poems, historical novels, and fantasy stories).

Besides the standards, the Young Reader app is a great tool for increasing media fluency skills to reflect students' understanding of the content. The app mixes the newest technology with proven teaching techniques that build good reading habits and optimal eye tracking. The app allows Jordan and other students to follow along as the guide leads them through the text to incrementally increase their reading speed (figure 2.20). Using the guide, similar to following along a line of text with a pen or your finger, is a technique taught in speed reading classes around the world.

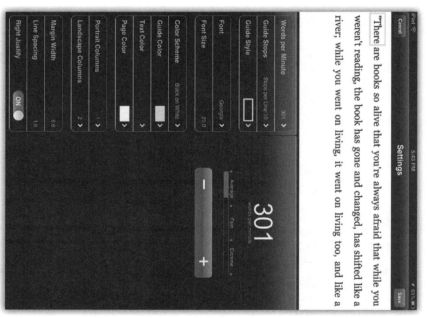

Figure 2.20—Young Reader text guide/reading speed indicator

Teachers can use Young Reader in the classroom on the iPod Touch or iPad to improve their students' reading skills. There is also an option to import text from other sources. This app is a great learning intervention tool for those who need a bit of extra help getting up to speed (literally) with their peers. The 130-plus books preloaded on Young Reader are also available offline, so there is no need for Wi-Fi or 3G Internet access to read the books, making it perfect for the classroom without wireless Internet. This app can be the encouragement young readers need to become better acquainted with contemporary books with outstanding literary appeal. With Instapaper text from web pages, long articles or blog posts can be added to Young Reader for reading later. With the iBookshelf app, users can search for books online to add to Young Reader. There are also Spanish, French, and German versions of the app.

What Happened? (Book Reading Apps)

The book reading applications not only work to increase students' reading speed, but also to introduce them to complex text. This is something the Common Core State Standards want students to be able to do. Students can practice the reading speed skills at any time with books they can carry around in their backpacks or pockets.

Tools for Literacy: Apps in the Spotlight

Name(s): Book Creator for iPad

Cost: $4.99

iTunes URL(s): http://bit.ly/OMMURo

Type: Books

Device: iPad

Description: Book Creator offers a simple way to create beautiful books, right on the iPad. Teachers and students can read them in iBooks, send them to others through email, or they can be submitted to the iBookstore. Book Creator is ideal for people creating books with a few interactive tools, including recorded voice, imported audio, and music. An upcoming free upgrade includes adding video to books.

Name: Dictionary / Dictionary without Ads

Cost: Free / $4.99

iTunes URL: http://bit.ly/PGLJQb

Type: Reference

Device: iPad / iPod Touch / iPhone

Description: The free Dictionary.com app delivers trusted reference content from Dictionary.com and Thesaurus.com. The app includes nearly two million words, definitions, synonyms, and antonyms. It also features audio pronunciation, voice-to-text search, and Dictionary.com's popular Word of the Day and Hot Word blogs.

Name: Drawing Pad

Cost: $1.99

iTunes URL: http://bit.ly/N6MOIQ

Type: Entertainment

Device: iPad

Description: Drawing Pad is a virtual mobile art studio designed exclusively for the iPad. The beautiful user interface puts the fun into creating art. Students can create their own art using "actual-sized" photo-realistic crayons, markers, paint brushes, colored pencils, stickers, roller pens, and more. Art can be saved to iPhoto or shared via email, Twitter, or Facebook.

Name: Grammar Express Parts of Speech, Tenses, Active and Passive Voice, Nouns HD

Cost: $2.99 iPad / $1.99 iPod Touch/iPhone

iTunes URL: http://bit.ly/s251Yb

Type: Education

Device: iPad / iPod Touch / iPhone

Description: Grammar Express is an app that helps users to learn English grammar rules. Each rule is explained by several examples followed by test questions.

Name: iBooks

Cost: Free

iTunes URL: http://bit.ly/MC2VqC

Type: Books

Device: iPad / iPod Touch / iPhone

Description: iBooks is an amazing way to download and read books. iBooks includes the iBookstore, where users can download the latest best-selling books or favorite classics—day or night. Browse the library on a beautiful bookshelf, tap a book to open it, flip through pages with a swipe or a tap, and bookmark or add notes to favorite passages. Books can now be created on a Mac computer or using OpenOffice on the PC. Word documents can be uploaded to sites like www.2epub.com, where the document is converted to an epub document for downloading. Updates to the app also allow users to read documents created in iBooks Author, a free tool for Mac computers that allows users to create unique interactive ebooks.

Name: iLiveGrammar Botany, Autumn, and Winter

Cost: $4.99

iTunes URL: http://bit.ly/rwMZso

Type: Education

Device: iPad / iPod Touch / iPhone

Description: All the iLiveGrammar apps available on the iTunes store, including Botany, Winter, and Autumn, use randomly generated sentences to test grammar while results are tracked. The results can then be sent by email to teachers and parents.

Name: My Spelling Test

Cost: $0.99

iTunes URL: http://bit.ly/QG49EF

Type: Education

Device: iPad / iPod Touch / iPhone

Description: My Spelling Test was designed so that students could make tests and practice on their own. It's a breeze to add words, take tests, and see scores. After each test, their scores and which words were misspelled are saved. Even if students practice by themselves, you can always see how well they did each time they took the test.

Name: PuppetPals HD

Cost: Free / $2.99 for Director's Pass

iTunes URL: http://bit.ly/Ovdkal

Type: Entertainment

Device: iPad

Description: Create unique shows with animation and audio in real time. Simply pick out actors and backdrops, drag them to the stage, and tap record. Movements and audio will be recorded in real time for playback later. Act out a story of pirates on the high seas, fight as scary monsters, or play the part of a Wild West bandit on the loose. With the full version of the app, students can add their own characters and choose from twelve other sets of characters, including politicians and talk show hosts. Students' creations are limited only by their imagination.

Name: SpellBoard / Spellboard Buddy

Cost: Free / $4.99 for full version

iTunes URL: SpellBoard— http://bit.ly/PqySkM /
Spellboard Buddy— http://bit.ly/OEM2w8

Type: Education

Device: iPad / iPod Touch / iPhone

Description: SpellBoard provides a fast and intuitive way for students (or teachers) to enter their own lists of spelling words. All they need to do is enter the word (correctly spelled), their grade level (1–12), and the spoken word (recorded via the iPad's built-in microphone). Optionally, they can add a written and/or spoken phrase. Now students are ready to study their word lists and be quizzed on them. SpellBoard allows for multiple student profiles, so teachers can track the performance of any student across a number of quizzes. SpellBoard also has a study mode that enables students to walk through a quiz seeing and hearing the words and phrases.

Name: StoryKit

Cost: Free

iTunes URL: http://bit.ly/M7IBIe

Type: Education

Device: iPad / iPod Touch / iPhone

Description: StoryKit enables users to create an electronic storybook. Students can make use of the little gaps in life—on the sofa after dinner, in the back seat of the car, or on a train—to do something creative. Sounds can be recorded for telling stories or as sound effects. Lay out the elements of a story (text boxes, images, and sound clips) freely by dragging them or pinching to resize.

Name: Young Reader

Cost: $4.99

iTunes URL: http://bit.ly/Mgpcc5

Type: Books

Device: iPad / iPod Touch / iPhone

Description: Make learning, studying, and reading more fun for kids with the Young Readers' edition of QuickReader. A highly customizable eBook reader and speed reading coach all in one, it teaches kids proper reading and eye tracking skills, and comes preloaded with more than 130 classic children's books. Teachers can use it in the classroom on the iPod Touch and iPad to improve their students' reading skills. It's not just for the advanced readers in the class; it's also a great learning intervention tool for those who need a bit of extra help getting up to speed (literally) with their peers.

Chapter 3

Tools for Social Studies

3 Tools for Social Studies

This chapter explores how applications can be used in a social studies classroom. The apps selected primarily focus on United States history and geography and include information on historical events, people, and places. The applications detailed here are This Day in History by World Book, The Civil War Today, U.S. Geography by Discovery Education, The World Factbook for iPad, USA Factbook and Quiz, and Wikihood Plus for iPad.

History Today and Yesterday: Social Studies in Focus

What happened 20, 50, or 100 years ago, and what impact does it have on what's happening today? Using the This Day In History by World Book app, users can click to view important events and people who have played important roles in the history of the world.

Why is an app like This Day in History needed in a social studies classroom? Middle school students can be a part of active learning by looking at the event that happened or the person who was born on This Day in History and engaging in reflective thinking about that event or person and why this app sees this person or event as important. Students can develop new understanding through a process of active construction of knowledge. This active construction is information fluency. They can ask good questions about historical facts and analyze the data, turning it into usable knowledge. October 13, for example, is the birthday of Margaret Thatcher (figure 3.1).

Jordan can research Margaret Thatcher and how she became her party's leader, and he can distinguish between good and bad and fact and opinion regarding how events he may be studying in social studies are connected with her. He can ask questions such as, "Did this person really influence anything that is relevant to things that we are doing today?"

A great feature of the app is samples of an individual's works. As an example, folk musician Paul Simon is listed in the app along with a sampling of his music. Students can listen by clicking on his name, and then answer questions about him.

Figure 3.1—This Day in History: Margaret Thatcher's birthday

An example question to quickly get background information might be, "What is folk music and what does the music of Simon and Garfunkel say about the 60s in the United States and the world?" Students may find an interest in folk music after listening to the sample.

The app also includes important speeches from U.S. presidents and other historical figures. The This Day in History app can be a starting point in the social studies classroom to assist learners with exploring and asking questions about the nature of world cultures in different places, times, conditions, and contexts.

The Civil War Today

Figure 3.2—The Civil War Today app explores Simon Cameron

The apps in this chapter enable learners to identify and describe significant historical periods. The Civil War Today app (figure 3.2) can guide students using critical historical inquiry to reconstruct and interpret the past using a variety of sources and checking their credibility.

Features of The Civil War Today include biographies, glossary, and search features. The Day in the Life writings include descriptions of events happening at the time as well as the dialogue Americans used 150 years ago. Students can draw evidence from the informational texts in The Civil War Today app to support analysis, reflection, and research.

What Happened? (This Day in History and The Civil War Today)

These apps provide an easy and quick connection for students to the world around them. There are many social studies apps similar to these that are about specific time periods. The Civil War Today app makes everything seem like real time because users cannot get ahead of today's date. Students can also tag different Civil War events with other things that were happening during the 1860s. The This Day in History app also allows for the connection of past events with current events. The speeches and music are great additions you will not get from a textbook.

People and Places—Geography Focus

U.S. Geography by Discovery Education is an app that allows students to research events of today as well as U.S. regional overviews, which include climate, culture, landforms, and major cities in the regions. Students can engage in activities prior to taking on the challenges about the different regions of the United States (figures 3.3 and 3.4).

Figures 3.3 and 3.4—The U.S. Geography app showing options for the Southwest region

The app allows users to study the seven different regions of the United States, and it includes audio and video resources in its activities. Another useful activity to prepare students for the challenges is to do an overview question before leaving the section.

Nations Standards for Social Studies Covered

Teachers of the middle grades can assist learners with exploring and asking questions about the nature of a culture that will allow for more in-depth study of the specific aspects of a particular culture in similar and different places, times, conditions, and contexts.

The U.S. Geography app has challenge questions, such as Landforms, that ask about things such as why people settled in the gulf coastal plains of Texas or why houses are built on stilts in the Galveston, Texas, area (figure 3.5).

Figure 3.5—U.S. Geography answers list

The study of geography allows learners to develop an understanding of the spatial contexts of people, places, and environments. It provides knowledge of Earth's physical and human systems and the interdependency of living things and physical environments. Studying geography stimulates curiosity the world's diverse inhabitants and places, as well as about local, regional, and global issues.

The U.S. Geography app allows learners to understand and make decisions about issues at the global level as well as the local level.

The World Factbook for iPad

The World Factbook app (figure 3.6) gives students and teachers extensive information on more than 250 countries and locations throughout the world. If students need to know about a specific country, see a world map, or make a comparison between different aspects of a country (which also encompasses math), this app provides the information.

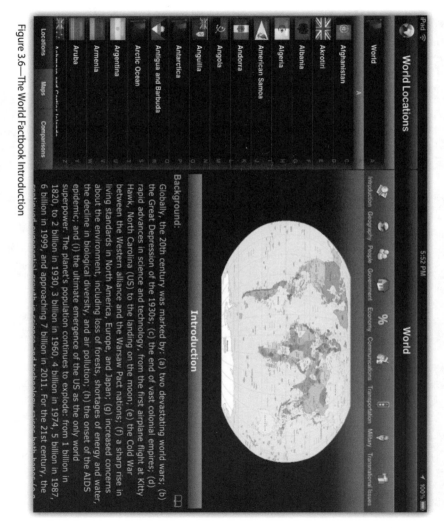

Figure 3.6—The World Factbook Introduction

There is an abundance of informational text to help students understand a country's economics. Cross-curricular activities could take place with an English classroom, with comparing and contrasting topics about different countries or areas around the world. Jordan can research natural resources in Angola, discovering that petroleum is its number one industry and learning why crude oil is its number one export.

When investigating the different aspects of a country or location, students can click on an economy listed in the app to enhance their understanding, or they can tap on any word to get a quick definition.

In a middle school math classroom where students have to understand place value and decimals, the country comparisons could be used to teach math through social studies (figure 3.7). Students could use comparisons between countries throughout the world to enhance math skills.

Figure 3.7 — Country Comparisons

Country Comparisons

Geography — People

Area	Rank	Country	(sq km)	Date
Population	1	Russia	17,098,242	NA
Population growth rate	2	Canada	9,984,670	NA
Birth rate	3	United States	9,826,675	NA
Death rate	4	China	9,596,961	NA
Net migration rate	5	Brazil	8,514,877	NA
Infant mortality rate	6	Australia	7,741,220	NA
Life expectancy at birth	7	India	3,287,263	NA
Total fertility rate	8	Argentina	2,780,400	NA
HIV/AIDS - adult prevalence rate	9	Kazakhstan	2,724,900	NA
HIV/AIDS - people living with HIV/AIDS	10	Algeria	2,381,741	NA
HIV/AIDS - deaths	11	Congo, Democratic Republic of the	2,344,858	NA
Education expenditures	12	Greenland	2,166,086	NA
Economy	13	Saudi Arabia	2,149,690	NA
GDP (purchasing power parity)	14	Mexico	1,964,375	NA
GDP real growth rate	15	Indonesia	1,904,569	NA
	16	Sudan	1,861,484	NA
	17	Libya	1,759,540	NA
	18	Iran	1,648,195	NA
	19	Mongolia	1,564,116	NA
	20	Peru	1,285,216	NA

Locations   Maps   Comparisons

Figure 3.7—The World Factbook country comparisons

Students could also solve teacher-created problems from the app; for example, the percentage of the population of a country with mobile phones. Ratio problems could be derived from unemployment rates, labor forces, education expenditures, and more.

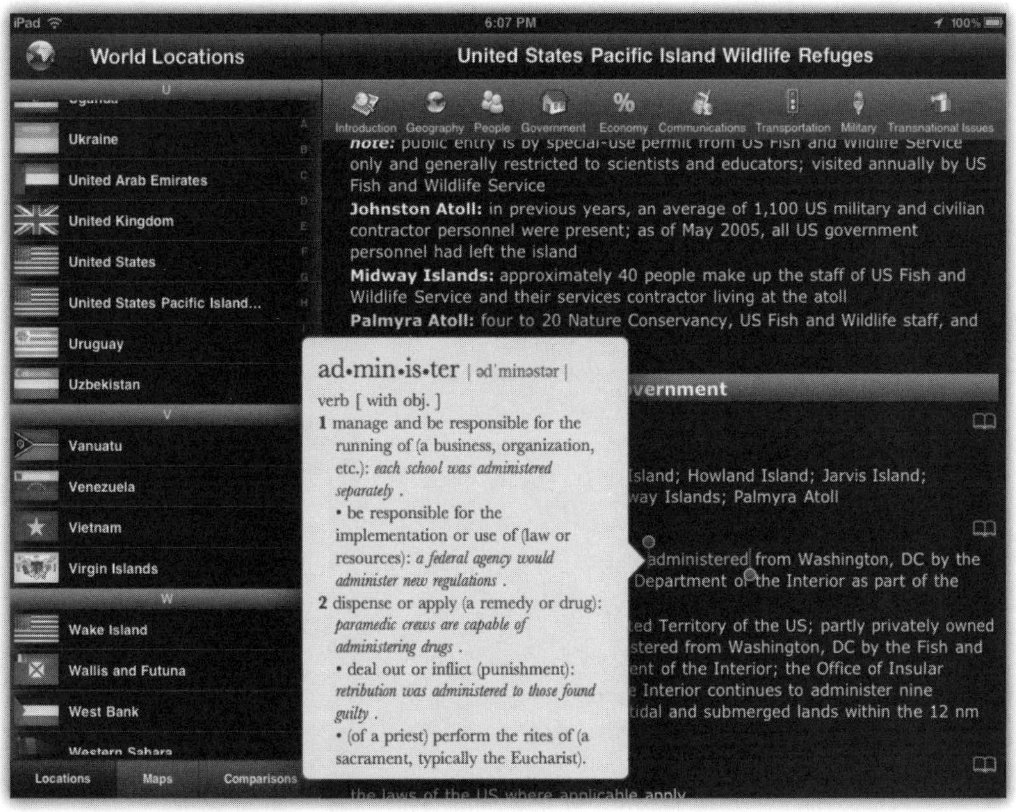

Figure 3.8 — United States Pacific Island Wildlife Refuges

World Locations

U
Ukraine
United Arab Emirates
United Kingdom
United States
United States Pacific Island...
Uruguay
Uzbekistan

V
Vanuatu
Venezuela
Vietnam
Virgin Islands

W
Wake Island
Wallis and Futuna
West Bank
Western Sahara

United States Pacific Island Wildlife Refuges

note: public entry is by special-use permit from US Fish and Wildlife Service only and generally restricted to scientists and educators; visited annually by US Fish and Wildlife Service

Johnston Atoll: in previous years, an average of 1,100 US military and civilian contractor personnel were present; as of May 2005, all US government personnel had left the island

Midway Islands: approximately 40 people make up the staff of US Fish and Wildlife Service and their services contractor living at the atoll

Palmyra Atoll: four to 20 Nature Conservancy, US Fish and Wildlife staff, and

ad·min·is·ter | ədˈminstər |
verb [with obj.]
1 manage and be responsible for the running of (a business, organization, etc); *each school was administered separately*.
• be responsible for the implementation or use of (law or resources): *a federal agency would administer new regulations*.
2 dispense or apply (a remedy or drug): *paramedic crews are capable of administering drugs*.
• deal out or inflict (punishment): *retribution was administered to those found guilty*.
• (of a priest) perform the rites of (a sacrament, typically the Eucharist).

Locations   Maps   Comparisons

Figure 3.8—The World Factbook spotlight on wildlife refuges

The World Factbook for iPad is an app that receives constant updates to keep the content relevant (figure 3.8), which makes this an app that always has current information for a long shelf life.

USA Factbook and Quiz

If you are a social studies or civics teacher looking for an app to help teach students about what it means to be responsible participants in political life, the USA Factbook and Quiz app (figure 3.9) is a great resource.

Not only do you get the original text of documents like the Declaration of Independence and the Articles of Confederation, you will also get background information about the documents. Using this app in civics and other government classes allows learners to find answers to the following questions:

- **What is civic life?**

- **What is politics?**

- **What is a government?**

- **What are the foundations of the American political system?**

- **How does the government of the United States, established by the Constitution, embody the purposes, values, and principles of American democracy?**

With hyperlinks to Wikipedia articles, biographies, and major cities information (figure 3.10), a wealth of social studies informational text is available within the app.

The USA Factbook and Quiz includes links to information about each of the 44 presidents (figure 3.11), 50 states, the national anthem and flag, eight geographical and historical maps, and information on the 100 largest cities in the country. Quizzes about states and their capitals are embedded in the app. Many of the social studies standards are addressed in the USA Factbook and Quiz app. Three social studies standards are listed here that this app addresses:

- Students shall develop an understanding of the forms and roles of government.

- Students shall develop an understanding of the rights and responsibilities of citizens. Determine the way rights and laws of the United States were created by examining founding documents (e.g., the Declaration of Independence, the United States Constitution, and the Mayflower Compact).

- Evaluate the importance of the United States Constitution as a governing document for the United States.

Figure 3.9—USA Factbook and Quiz menu

Figure 3.10—Information on New York City

Figure 3.11—Information on presidents

Wikihood Plus for iPad

With Wikihood Plus for iPad, students can learn about interesting sites nearby or far away. Students will find a wealth of information about museums, castles, government buildings, schools, and famous persons connected with these places, including political figures. The app combines geographic data with Wikipedia data and shows students important sites in their area as well as famous people who may be linked to their hometown. Within seconds of entering a location in the Wikihood app, a list of popular sites and information for that area can be viewed. By opening the app and clicking on their current location, students will quickly see information about the area around them and also how far they are from the given site.

When looking at the city of Little Rock, Arkansas, you can see Little Rock Central High is an important landmark (figure 3.12). After tapping on the historical place on the screen, you will get Wikipedia information on the site. With a click of the back button on the app, users can scroll up the page to find people who are linked to Central High School in some form or fashion. For example, President Dwight D. Eisenhower sent troops to escort nine black students into Little Rock Central High School, an all white public school, in the 1950s.

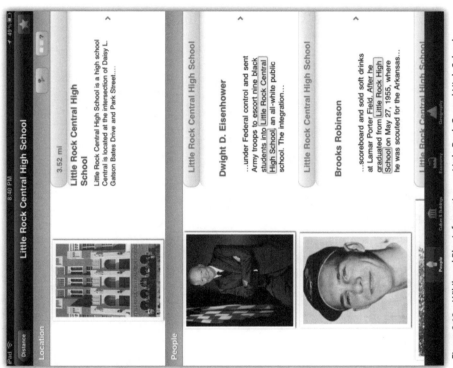

Figure 3.12—Wikihood Plus information on Little Rock Central High School

Houston Nutt, a coach for several university football programs (figure 3.13), graduated from the school. Joe Johnson, who played on a U.S. national basketball team and now plays for the Boston Celtics, attended Central High School also.

The app is always current, so any new facts or changes are reflected in the app. At the bottom of the screen, students can choose from people, culture, buildings, economy, and geography about an area. The app also allows the user to type in the name of a location.

Jordan was doing research on Pilgrims. He typed "Plymouth Massachusetts" in the search window and got information about the Pilgrims and current information about the city of Plymouth (figure 3.14).

Figure 3.13—Little Rock Central High School sports stars

He gets lots of information from the year 1620 and the Plymouth Plantation—a living museum about the city—and Squanto, who helped the Pilgrims during their first visit to North America. A map feature is also in the app, giving Jordan the top ten most important sites around the Plymouth area. Is there something geographically interesting in the proximity? Did a historic battle happen at this place? It's all right there in Wikihood Plus for iPad.

What Happened? (People and Places)

All of the apps in this chapter share facts about our history, but unlike printed texts, the history in these applications can change at a day's notice because updates happen quickly. The U.S. Geography app includes current news stories, along with maps of the event's location. This is authentic learning that can be incorporated into a social studies classroom.

The World Factbook also gives data that is updated regularly. It is not as current as the U.S. Geography app, but you will get information on more than 250 countries that is more current than hard copy textbooks we had to rely on in the classroom just a few years ago. Besides historical facts, the USA Factbook and Quiz app includes complex readings that the Common Core State Standards insist that students need.

Figure 3.14—All about Plymouth, Massachusetts

Wikihood also makes learning relevant to where students are because of location services built in the iPad, so they can easily find history around them. With the Wikihood Plus app, students can input different places to find out more about the location and its culture. The Wikihood Plus app is a great "take me on vacation" app because of its interactive features.

Tools for Social Studies: Apps in the Spotlight

Name: The Civil War Today

Cost: $5.99

iTunes URL: http://bit.ly/OMNChz

Type: Entertainment/education

Device: iPad

Description: The Civil War Today app allows the user to follow the events that happened 150 years ago over the next four years from April 12, 2011 through April 26, 2015. The app features a Day in the Life of fifteen historical figures such as Abraham Lincoln and Horatio Nelson Taft.

Name: This Day in History

Cost: Free

iTunes URL: http://bit.ly/RfWGZ

Type: History education

Device: iPad

Description: This free app is an interactive calendar that displays historical events for the current day or any selected day. The interactive elements are photos, illustrations, music, and speeches. New in this edition is one illustration or photograph for every event, as well as a paragraph or two on each topic taken from the 2011 World Book Encyclopedia.

Name: USA Factbook and Quiz

Cost: $0.99

iTunes URL: http://bit.ly/Npxdvm

Type: Education

Device: iPad / iPod Touch / iPhone

Description: This app features the most important U.S. documents, including the Declaration of Independence, Articles of Confederation, and the Constitution with amendments and the Bill of Rights. The app includes facts on all fifty states, all U.S. presidents, and the 100 most populated cities.

Name: U.S. Geography by Discovery Education

Cost: $6.99

iTunes URL: http://bit.ly/PqzlnI

Type: Education

Device: iPad / iPod Touch / iPhone

Description: A very exciting way to discover the United States, with more than 700 different activities and forty-two embedded content videos and questions that allow you to rank against the rest of the world through a Facebook connection. The app includes Discovery News stories that are updated frequently and address topics such as the Earth, archaeology, and dinosaurs. These stories also coincide with current events.

Name: Wikihood Plus for iPad

Cost: $6.99

iTunes URL: http://bit.ly/OvebrV

Type: Travel

Device: iPad

Description: Wikihood Plus for iPad provides answers to the following questions:

- What are the most important sights to see around me?

- What do others find interesting here?

- Is there a museum, a castle, a park, or church nearby?

- What persons are connected with this place?

- What are the most important companies here?

- Is there something geographically interesting in the proximity?

- Did a historic battle happen at this place?

Name: World Factbook for iPad

Cost: $1.99

iTunes URL: http://bit.ly/MmR7xd

Type: Education

Device: iPad

Description: A very exciting way to discover more than 250 countries and locations around the world. There are three different ways to discover information—by location, maps, and comparisons. When searching by location, there are nine different topics covered, including government, economy, and military. The app receives periodic updates, which makes it an enhancement to any social studies classroom.

Chapter 4

Tools for Mathematics

4 Tools for Mathematics

Sam is a middle school mathematics teacher. Her classroom is a dynamic and active space with the students engaged and motivated to learn. Sam uses a variety of teaching approaches ranging from traditional instruction to blended and self-directed learning.

Road Safety—A Mathematical Investigation

Sam's seventh-grade mathematics class is working on a project about road safety. Sam has designed the project to be relevant and to have a real-world context for the students solving a real and pressing problem the community faces. The students and staff had wondered how fast cars were traveling past the front gates of the school. While the speed limit is 30 mph, they suspected that the cars frequently exceed this. The students were charged with designing an investigation that collected information about the speed of cars passing the school, and then presenting their findings and recommendations to the class.

The students used the 6D's framework of Solution Fluency to structure and plan the task. The process was as follows:

Define the task: The students need to collect suitable data about the speed of the cars passing the school to make informed recommendations about the safety of the students and families of the school community. The teacher made this a checkpoint to ensure the students understood the task. The students wrote the definition and core concept they were investigating using iThoughtsHD. This app is a mind mapping, or graphical organizer, tool the students will use to organize their ideas. Once they have the main ideas down, they then elaborate on them. The final part of constructing the mind map is building the relationships between the different elements or concepts. iThoughtsHD includes icons for Edward DeBono's Six Thinking Hats, allowing it to be easily used to consider these different elements and concepts.

This is a simple template set up in iThoughtsHD (figure 4.1) to allow the students to work through Edward DeBono's Six Thinking Hats. The students start a new map based upon the one they want to use as a template.

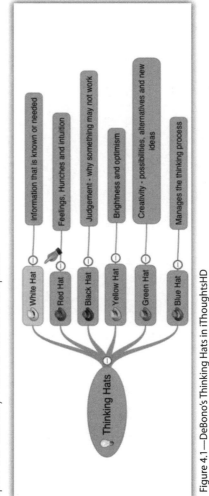

Figure 4.1—DeBono's Thinking Hats in iThoughtsHD

Discover the background: The students developed a list of key questions they outlined in their mind maps. They investigated the local bylaws about speed restrictions around schools and school bus services. They also investigated what speed is and discovered the formula for speed (distance covered per unit of time) from their science teacher. The students used the Safari web browser to access the local council websites and Maps to find maps of the school area they could use. Using the mind map to construct the questions prior to starting the research means the time spent using search engines on the browser is purposeful and deliberate. It provides a useful scaffold for their primary research. They have already developed the questions before they ask their science teacher about the topic. The students then update their mind maps with the answers.

The students used iThoughtsHD to develop their mind map below (figure 4.2).

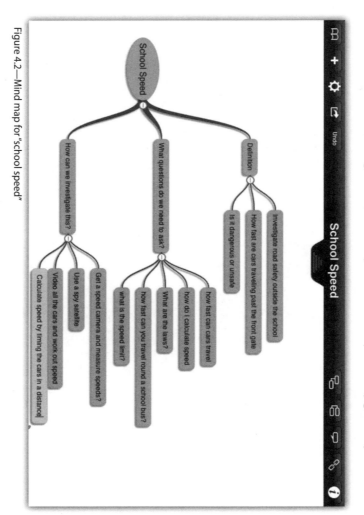

Figure 4.2—Mind map for "school speed"

Dream about a solution: As a group, the students brainstormed ideas about how they could investigate speeds. The students used iThoughtsHD to mind map the ideas. The process they used was a blue sky process where every member of the group contributed ways that they could measure the speed of the cars passing the school, no matter how far-fetched the idea was. One student was the facilitator for the task; she asked each person in turn for an idea and encouraged him or her to think outside the square. Concepts were not criticized, as each student was encouraged to suggest and propose a wide variety of different solutions to the problem. One student was given the task of being the recorder, and he entered the ideas into the mind map. Each idea was recorded as a different bubble on the mind map. Once all the students had contributed at least one idea, they went through an elimination process. This refined the concepts down to two that were feasible, and the group then selected which of the two they thought was most suitable for the task. At this point, they had to check in with the teacher before proceeding to the Design phase. This process allowed all students to contribute and be involved in the design of the solution.

Design the solution: The teacher had approved the students' concept and set the next checkpoint for them, which was to design the investigation. The students planned to measure and mark a section of the road in front of the school gates and time the cars as they traveled between the road cones.

The data, which is raw facts and figures, would be recorded in Numbers to make it easy to translate into processed data. The students used several columns in which they recorded key information, such as time taken, time of day, and car details, and then used a formula they had created to calculate the speed of the cars.

To help make their evidence more compelling, they would record some of the cars passing the gates using the built-in camera in the iPad. They would then use iMovie (figure 4.3) to edit clips showing a car traveling safely below the speed limit, at the speed limit, and exceeding the speed limit, as well as to add annotations and estimations of speed.

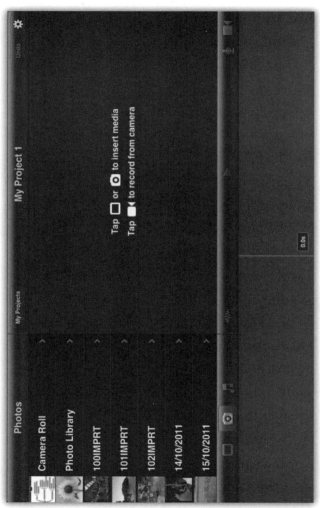

Figure 4.3—iMovie in action

They planned to bring the video evidence and information together in a keynote presentation, displaying the speeds of the vehicles in a graph. The students debated what sort of graph they would use. They considered a pie graph, which would show the proportion of cars at different speeds. They dismissed a line graph as this is for continuous data and would not suit the information they were collecting. Scattergrams were dismissed as well; while they could be used to show both speed and the number of cars, it was harder to see trends clearly. They eventually decided that a bar graph would best display the information they needed. Students were asked to justify their selection of graphs based on the data they had. They were also asked if further processing and organization of data was required to clearly explain the trends they had seen.

This is using Higher Order Thinking or HOTS. The students will be analyzing (breaking down into component parts) and evaluating (making judgements). They will calculate the average speed of the cars; the proportions of cars above, below, or at the speed limit; the range of speeds they observed; and the maximum and minimum speeds. They will write the formulas in Numbers (figure 4.4).

Spreadsheets Undo			School Speed			
Sheet 1			+			
car #	Time	Speed in m/s	Speed in Km/hr	Speed Differenc		
1	1	15	54			
2	2	7.5	27			
3	2.5	6	21.6			
4	1.5	10	36			
5	2	7.5	27			
6	3	5	18			
7	4	3.75	13.5			
8	2	7.5	27			
9	1	15	54			
10	1.5	10	36			

Fig 4—Numbers spreadsheet for school speed

The fill function in Numbers, accessed by selecting the cell with a double tap, allows users to drag the function or formula across a range of cells. Once the data is in and suitably collated, the students will make conclusions and present their findings.

Do the experiment: The students measured out a section of the road. They used a 15m section and marked this with road cones. They then used a stopwatch to measure time and record this directly into their spreadsheet in Numbers. Once they had collected their data, they processed it by calculating the following:

• Average speed

• Maximum speed

• Minimum speed

• Range

• Number of cars sampled

This information was then processed into a bar graph. They processed the captured video and selected representative clips for the cars below, at, and above the speed limit. They annotated these with suitable keynote graphics. The students selected the graph that best represents the data they had collected (figure 4.5).

The students were surprised to find that most cars were either at or below the speed limit, and they thought that they had failed in their task. However, Sam pointed out that this was

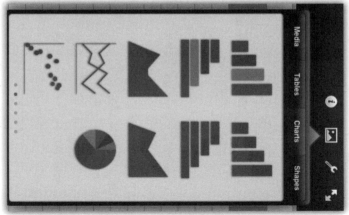

Figure 4.5—Numbers graph options

an excellent result, and that they had to present a conclusion based on their findings. She pointed out that not all investigations report a negative result (figure 4.6).

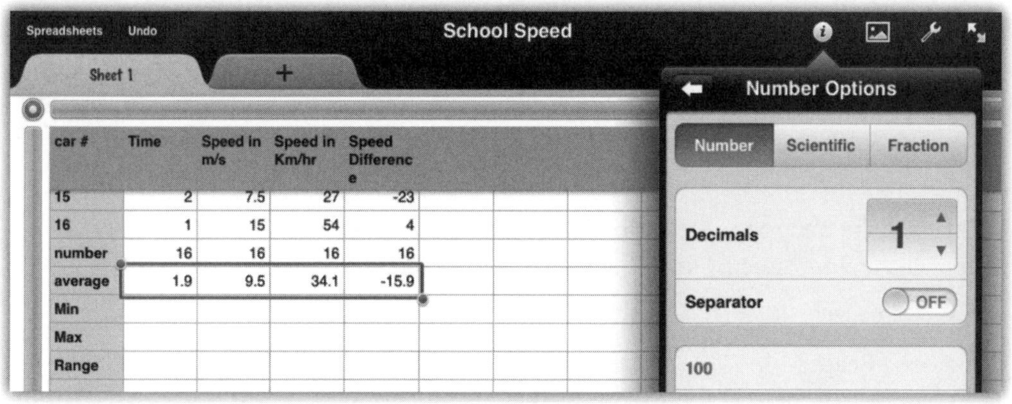

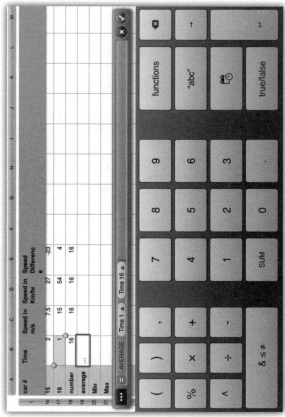

Figure 4.6—The students format the numbers to one decimal place

Debrief the process: The students reflected on discovering that their result meant no actual change was required. They had been disappointed in finding this result, but this was a great opportunity for the students to understand that not all investigations or experiments will end in success or in the result that they expect. The students also considered the changes and improvements they could make. They decided on the following:

• Collect a larger sample of car speeds to ensure that they had a representative sample

• Collect the information at different times of the day and days of the week to get a better estimation of speed of the vehicles

• Have a longer sample distance to more accurately measure time

The students developed a formula based around the built-in functions. They selected a range of cells to be processed, and they used a full colon (:) to represent *to* and *from*. So this formula calculates the average from cell Time 1 to cell Time 16 (figure 4.7).

Figure 4.7—Calculating average times

Textbooks Online and Beyond

Pauline is a physically small student in Grade 6. Every day she brings to school and takes home her mathematics and other textbooks, her exercise books, physical education gear, and more. Her school bag is laden and heavy. For many of the younger students, the weight of their bags is a considerable ergonomic issue. However, many of the mathematics textbooks come with an electronic version, and there are reference resources the students can use that reduce and lighten the load.

Many of the electronic versions of the textbooks are in PDF, a standard format that can be opened and accessed by many applications on the iPad. These include:

- Goodreader
- Adobe Reader
- iBooks

PDF versions of textbooks are essentially limited electronic duplications. They lack any interactivity and are not particularly engaging. While they do reduce the weight in a student's bag, they do little for mathematics as a fun and exciting field of endeavor and learning.

Apple's recent release of iBooks Author—a free epub authoring tool available on Apple laptops and desktops—makes it considerably easier to develop electronic resources including extensive color images, hyperlinks, and other media. Teachers are no longer restricted to creating either paper-based versions of resources or saving in PDF format files. They can now add increased interactivity to the materials they develop for their students. These files can be accessed via iBooks on the iPad.

One of the tools that Sam uses with her students is Sketchpad Explorer. It is an interactive, challenging, and versatile app. Sam's students use Sketchpad Explorer to develop a basic understanding of the mathematical concepts of geometry, algebra, and elementary mathematics. It allows the students to dig deeper into the wonders of mathematics. The students enjoy being able to manipulate the objects (figure 4.8) and receive instant feedback.

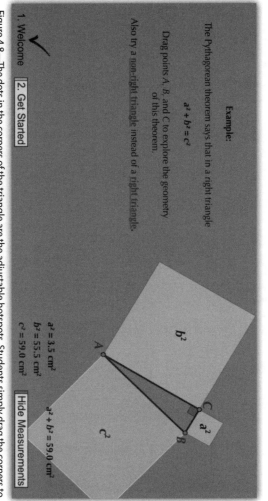

1. Welcome | **2. Get Started**

Example:

The Pythagorean theorem says that in a right triangle

$$a^2 + b^2 = c^2$$

Drag points A, B, and C to explore the geometry of this theorem.

Also try a non-right triangle instead of a right triangle.

$a^2 = 3.5 \text{ cm}^2$
$b^2 = 55.5 \text{ cm}^2$
$c^2 = 59.0 \text{ cm}^2$

$a^2 + b^2 = 59.0 \text{ cm}^2$

b^2

c^2

a^2

Hide Measurements

Figure 4.8—The dots in the corners of the triangle are the adjustable hotspots. Students simply drag the corners to increase and decrease the lengths of the sides of the triangle.

To develop an understanding of frequency or period and amplitude on a graph, the application uses the example of a sound wave. The students visualize this on a graph and listen to the resulting changes in pitch and volume as they shorten and lengthen the frequency and increase and decrease the amplitude (figure 4.9). Sam's classroom is awash with low frequency bass tones and high frequency squeals as the students are actively engaged in learning.

Figure 4.9—Changing amplitude/frequency by dragging the X into different positions

The resources in Sketchpad Explorer are arranged in tabs, making it easy for students to work through and return to the interactive elements time and time again to reinforce their learning. Graphs can be manipulated by dragging the value on the axis. Sketchpad Explorer also has resources for algebra, geometry, and elementary mathematics.

The use of interactive elements adds to the students' engagement in the learning process. Learning becomes a multisensory process, and the addition of each sensory layer enhances this process. Students manipulating these interactive features are learning in visual, auditory, and kinesthetic modes. When the students are asked to then verbalize their understanding, explaining it to their peers or their teacher, they have developed a much deeper and richer understanding.

In Sam's blended classroom, she moves easily from traditional teaching approaches to self-directed learning and extension. She expects the students to continue their learning at home. Her students have been provided with a Mathletics account and they use this online subscription to reinforce classroom learning, challenge themselves on fun mathematical games, and extend their learning (figure 4.10).

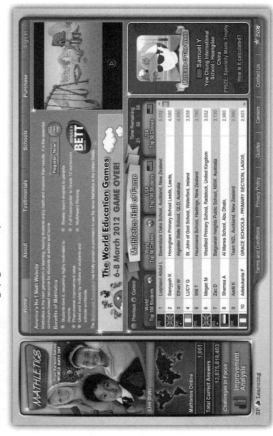

Figure 4.10—Mathletics home page

While Mathletics is a Flash-based online resource, the students are able to use the Rover or Puffin web browser, which supports Flash, to access these engaging resources. The Rover web browser was designed specifically for K–12 education and is the recommended product for schools. In addition to supporting Flash, it also has a content filtering system that provides a degree of protection. A number of key sites, such as Mathletics and the Discovery Channel, are preloaded into this browser.

Mathletics is a subscription-based web product that provides students with age-appropriate challenges that are engaging and fun. The students play in a game-based environment that provides regular feedback and reward. There is a healthy degree of competition allowing the top students to feature on the world or regional Hall of Fame. All students achieve a degree of success and are able to retake tests as required.

The teacher is able to control access to the material to match the teaching program. Teachers, students, and parents receive regular weekly updates of progress, and the students are rewarded with certificates for achieving the weekly goals. The bronze and silver certificates contribute to the highest award—the gold certificate.

Sam regularly sets her students learning tasks using MathBoard to reinforce basic number theory and mathematical process. The students test themselves against a series of randomly generated mathematical problems (figure 4.11) and receive immediate feedback.

Sam will set the parameters of what she wants the students to practice and the number range. She can set a range of operators that include:

- Addition
- Subtraction
- Multiplication
- Division
- Squares
- Cubes
- Square roots

Sam can set maximum and minimum values and also allow negative numbers. This flexibility makes MathBoard an excellent tool for reinforcement, and it's ideal for self-directed learning.

Sam is able to adjust the parameters to suit the development of the student and easily adjust these to extend and challenge them. Students set up their own accounts on their MathBoard app.

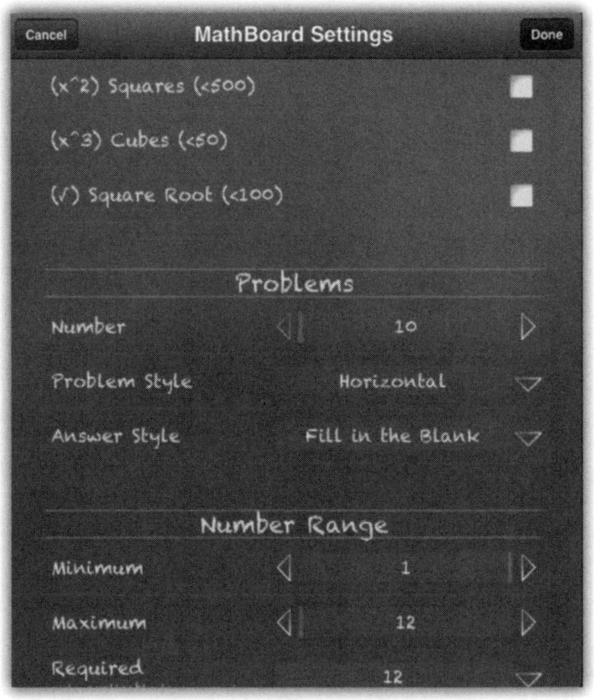

Figure 4.11—MathBoard problem examples

Sam encourages the students to use the Problem Solver space, a virtual chalkboard, to write out the problem and process (figure 4.12). Being able to visualize the mathematical process is a vital component of learning.

Students are encouraged to work not only for accuracy, but for speed as well. Sam motivates her students to be self-directed learners, and they make use of the Problem Solver, a tutorial element of the application, to support their learning and understanding. There are problem solvers for addition, subtraction, multiplication, and division, each taking the learner through a step-by-step process to work out the answer to the problem. MathBoard allows for the development of basic mathematical skills and their reinforcement in a fun, engaging, and varied testing environment.

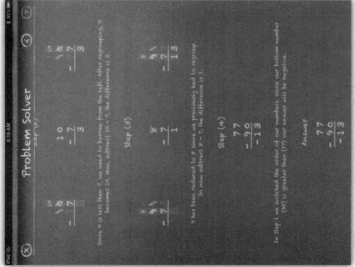

Figure 4.12—MathBoard Problem Solver

Measuring and Estimating—Field Protractor

Field Protractor is an application Sam likes to use with her students around the school (figure 4.13).

Figure 4.13—Field Protractor allows the learner to measure angles and add in a scale to calculate the dimensions of the objects. In this case, the building is a hotel on the waterfront in Singapore.

The students will wander around the school and use the camera on the iPad to take snapshots of the buildings. Then, using the protractor, they are able to measure the angles of those buildings. The students will take a tape measure with them and measure the length or aspect of the building and add this into the scale. The protractor then calculates the base line and angle arm length.

Sam uses this tool with her students to develop a practical understanding of angles and scale. Having made these calculations, the students are then able to calculate the areas and volumes of the different structures. The application allows the students to send the image with the embedded angles, lengths, and scale to an email recipient or to save it locally on the iPad for later use.

Tools for Mathematics: Apps in the Spotlight

Name: Field Protractor

Cost: $0.99

iTunes URL: http://bit.ly/PGPiWo

Type: Measurement and estimation tool

Device: iPad

Description: Field Protractor is an easy-to-use measurement and estimation tool. Students use images captured from the iPad's camera or from the photo container. They set the base and angle arm length to correspond with the dimensions of the object. They can then set and select the scale and calculate the length of the arms. Images with the protractor and measurements can be emailed to recipients and saved locally on the iPad.

Name: iMovie

Cost: $4.99

iTunes URL: http://bit.ly/OKSkOi

Type: Video editor

Device: iPad / iPhone

Description: iMovie is a video editor that uses the iPad's built-in camera by recording directly into the application or using images and video from the camera roll or photo container. The user can edit and manipulate the timeline and add transitions and keynote graphics. Music or narration can be added to the sound recorded with the video capture itself. The volume of the individual sound tracks can be increased or decreased as required. The finished product can be exported to a camera roll in 360p, 480p, and 720p HD formats, as well as shared to different locations including YouTube, Vimeo, and Facebook.

Name: MathBoard

Cost: $4.99

iTunes URL: http://bit.ly/RfHiI8

Type: Mathematical reinforcement and learning resource

Device: iPad

Description: MathBoard allows users to test and reinforce their understanding of basic mathematical processes and operations. The software includes tutorial elements that take the learner step by step through solving addition, subtraction, multiplication, and division problems. Learners are provided immediate feedback in the testing phase and are able to switch to the Problem Solver to show the process for solving that problem.

Name: Numbers

Cost: $9.99

iTunes URL: http://bit.ly/MmRpnC

Type: Spreadsheet and data processing

Device: iPad / iPod Touch / iPhone

Description: Numbers is a spreadsheet and data processing tool that allows the user to collate and process data and present it in tablular and graphic formats. The application has a wide range of functions that enable the user to process information and apply the process to a range of cells using the fill option. A large number of templates are available for different purposes, and users can also create their own. These templates are useful as they also show how formula, functions, and graphs can be effectively used in the spreadsheets. Files can be exported as XLS format files or in iWorks Numbers format.

Name: Sketchpad Explorer

Cost: Free

iTunes URL: http://bit.ly/RfHuAU

Type: Mathematical learning resource

Device: iPad

Description: Sketchpad Explorer is an interactive application with learning resources for various areas of mathematics. The resources contain interactive elements that allow students to manipulate and change the different variables, instantly visualizing the effect that each change causes. The pages are structured into a learning progression and supported by easy-to-follow and understandble text. The learning games are simple and engaging, reinforcing the mathematical concepts. Sketchpad Explorer has resources for geometry, algebra, and elementary mathematics.

Chapter **5**

Tools for
Science

5 Tools for Science

In this chapter, we will investigate how some applications can be used in the science classroom. The applications selected are the ones often used for day-to-day learning activities, including mind mapping/graphical organizers, word processors, and presentation tools. Some of the other applications are selected from the wealth of reference and simulation applications that bring the science classroom to life. The applications selected and detailed are Pages, iThoughts HD, Adobe Photoshop Express, Voicethread, Rat Dissection, Solar Walk, and the NASA app, to name a few.

Living with Rabbits—Life Science in Focus

Michelle is teaching her middle school science class. The class is studying life sciences and is developing an understanding of basic anatomy, food chains and webs, tropic levels, and ethical and responsible care for animals. The students in her class and her fellow teachers' classes are working in groups. Each group has a young rabbit that they are to care for. Throughout the course of this six-week unit, the students will look after the rabbit, recording its growth and developing a basic understanding of animal husbandry. For many of the students living in an urban environment, this represents a significant responsibility that they adopt with enthusiasm.

Keeping a Diary

One of the first tasks the students do is to create a diary of their daily interactions with their group's rabbit. They make regular notes on what they are doing and any changes they observe. The students are presented with a choice in how they make these notes.

Two methods are proposed and the students select which method suits them best. The first of the two methods is using the word processor Pages to create the journal (figure 5.1).

Figure 5.1—Rabbit diary in Pages

They add in a new paragraph each day and often use the iPad's built-in camera to take pictures and add these to the growing document. The students use Adobe Photoshop Express to edit the images. This allows the images to be cropped to a suitable size and then added to the document. While the content is more important, the students pay particular attention to the layout of their rabbit diary. Daily entries are formatted using the styles built into the word processor.

The second option suggested to the students was to create a mind map and brainstorm using iThoughts HD, which is a mind mapping or graphical organizer tool. The students created a new map each day, adding a new set of "daughter nodes" attached to the main concept (figure 5.2).

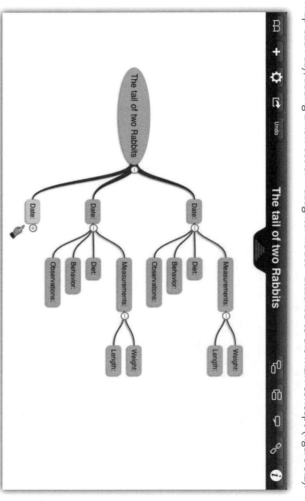

Figure 5.2—iThoughtsHD mind map "A Tail of Two Rabbits"

Figure 5.3—Adding images from the camera roll or photo library in Adobe Photoshop Express

Some students developed and used a template layout and pasted the daughter nodes into the mind map. Each entry into the mind map contained the students' observations of physical changes to their rabbit, dietary observations, behavioral comments, and so on. Some of the students used the smily icons to indicate if they felt their rabbit was happy, sad, or neutral. Students could have also used a tool like Popplet to create a mind map.

The students were able to add pictures they had taken either directly from the front or rear cameras or from the photos container (figure 5.3). The photos container has a number of basic editing features. Some students like to use the features in Adobe Photoshop Express to edit their images.

The key tools within this application are the rotate tool and the crop tool (figure 5.4). The composed images are added into a node and a caption can be easily added to each image. The pictures can be hidden or revealed by clicking on the + or - icons on the linking branch. Both Adobe and Apple offer advanced editing tools. Adobe Photoshop Touch and Apple's iPhoto are powerful image editors with a wide range of features to edit and manipulate images.

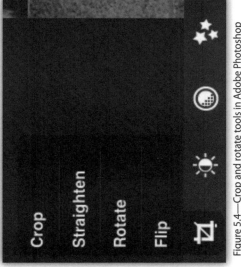

Figure 5.4—Crop and rotate tools in Adobe Photoshop Express

Collating and Processing the Data

As part of the unit, the students were required to collect and process data about the rabbit's growth and present this in a graphical form. The graph showing the animal's growth was added to the students' report. The students were shown how to use the spreadsheet tool in Numbers to enter, process, and present the data. They created columns labeled "date," "weight," and "length."

The students were expected to process the data to show average daily growth, overall growth, and length of observations. Some students added a fourth column that calculated the change in weight from day to day using a formula that subtracted that day's weight from the previous day's to give a daily change. Some of the students noticed a fluctuation in the weight of their animal and were initially concerned. However, when the rabbit's mass rapidly increased the next day, they realized the change was due to the rabbit's elimination of waste materials just before it was weighed.

The students organized and processed the raw data into usable form, and they were then able to see trends and present this data in suitable styles.

Understanding Anatomy

As the focus of one unit of learning was digestion, students used the virtual Rat Dissection app by PunFlay (figure 5.5) to develop an understanding of the digestive tract of a similar mammal. The students were able to manipulate the 3D models of the internal organs and use the screen capture/shot feature of the iPad to capture images of the organs. Pressing the Power and Home buttons together takes a screenshot and adds it to the photos container. The students edit this using either the editing tools in the photos container or using Adobe Photoshop Express. The images are then added to the documents or presentations the students are working on.

Figure 5.5—Rat Dissection home page

McREL Science—Life Sciences Standards at a Glance
Level 3 (Grades 6–8) Standard 6

Understands relationships among organisms and their physical environment

1. Knows that all individuals of a species that exist together at a given place and time make up a population, and all populations living together and the physical factors with which they interact compose an ecosystem.

2. Knows factors that affect the number and types of organisms an ecosystem can support (e.g., available resources; abiotic factors such as quantity of light and water, range of temperatures, and soil composition; disease; competition from other organisms within the ecosystem; predation).

3. Knows ways in which organisms interact and depend on one another through food chains and food webs in an ecosystem (e.g., producer/consumer; predator/prey; parasite/host, relationships that are mutually beneficial or competitive).

4. Knows how energy is transferred through food webs in an ecosystem (e.g., energy enters ecosystems as sunlight, and green plants transfer this energy into chemical energy through photosynthesis; this chemical energy is passed from organism to organism; animals get energy from oxidizing their food, releasing some of this energy as heat).

5. Knows how matter is recycled within ecosystems (e.g., matter is transferred from one organism to another repeatedly, and between organisms and their physical environment; the total amount of matter remains constant, even though its form and location change).

Walking on Different Worlds: Earth and Space Science in Focus

Mark is a seventh-grade science teacher. His class was conducting an investigation as part of their solar system project. The students in Mark's class were using the framework provide by Solution Fluency to present their understanding of the solar system. The students were presented with the essential question: "How could we develop methods to allow us to walk on different worlds?" The students were asked to investigate which planets in our solar system we could send astronauts to. Underlying this essential question and investigation were a number of foundation concepts.

These included:

- Developing an understanding of the solar system, planets, and celestial objects

- Investigating distance and speed in terms of astronomical units and conventional distance

- Understanding the capabilities and limitations of space travel currently in terms of craft, personnel, and survivability

- Understanding the basic requirements for life and relating these to current systems

- Investigating current space transport potential

Solving a Problem with Solution Fluency

The students were presented with the problem in the definition phase of the project. Solution Fluency has six phases that scaffold the students' progress and development. The fluency takes the students through the whole process, from defining a problem to creating a solution—in this case, a presentation—and, finally, debriefing from the task.

In the definition phase, the problem "investigate which planets in our solar system we could send astronauts to" is defined. The students understand that this is not a future problem being investigated, but an examination and report presenting both the potential and the limits of current manned space exploration. The scope of the project is deliberately designed to make the task manageable for the students. The students are to present their findings to the class in a digital format that they have selected. Their teacher has provided a number of suggestions, which include using a slideshow presentation tool such as iWorks Keynote, Prezi, Whiteboard HD, or VoiceThread (figure 5.6).

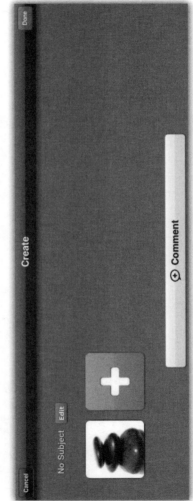

Figure 5.6.—The VoiceThread app allows you to insert media from your camera and add comments in either text or spoken formats

Voice Thread allows students to create a slideshow-style presentation, add their own captions, and record a narration for each slide. This is then shared online, and depending on the settings, viewers can leave voice comments to create a threaded discussion about the topic.

The students had access to a VGA adapter that allowed them to connect their devices to the projector in the classroom. Later in the investigation, the students were required to connect their devices to the projector and sound system and practice using the presentation tool. This also provided Mark with an opportunity to provide formative feedback to the students about their presentations, product design, and so on.

Structuring Their Learning

The students used iThoughtsHD, a mind mapping and graphical organization tool, to define the problem (figure 5.7). They were asked to consider the limitations and boundaries of the task and were provided with the assessment rubric for the different components and phases.

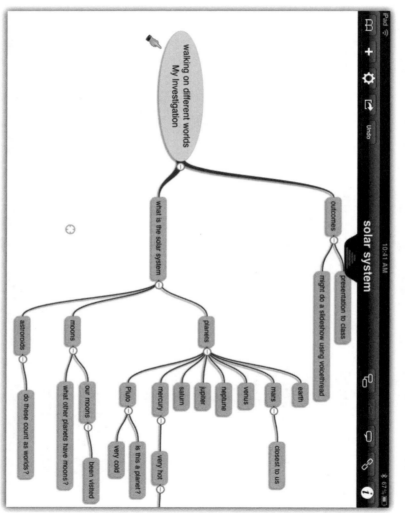

Figure 5.7—iThoughtsHD mind map for "Walking on Different Worlds"

Some of the students used this to collate the information they had collected from various secondary sources. Other students preferred to use a word processor, such as iWorks Pages or Quickoffice, for this purpose. In the discovery phase, the students needed to find out about which planets were in our solar system, their relative sizes, and their positions. They also examined the information available about the environmental conditions on the planets, background information on space travel, and current travel systems. The students also considered the requirements for human life in terms of food, water, air, and companionship. Some students also considered ethical considerations such as one-way and return flights.

Looking Up—Star Gazing Online

The students had access to a number of reference applications on their devices that they could use to gather secondary research. The first and most useful application for the task was the NASA app (figure 5.8), a free reference and news tool.

The students were able to look up specific information on the planets within the solar system from a valid and reliable source. The application also provided them with access to considerably more information than just celestial bodies.

Figure 5.8—NASA app showing the solar system

The NASA application shows the different celestial bodies. The students click on a planet; hyperlinks to asteroids, comets, and meteors; or the universe link to view even more detailed information.

The students were also able to access the collection of images and video resources that are available at www.nasaimages.org, as well as receive up-to-date information on missions, countdown clocks, and launch information.

The other reference applications the students had were Solar Walk and Star Walk. Both applications are produced by Vito Technologies. Star Walk allows users to point their enabled devices at the sky and see stars, constellations, and satellites in real time. Solar Walk has a closer focus in touring and examining our solar system.

Solar Walk has detailed information about the different planets and specifically the moons that have been identified. The students were able to use these reference applications to discover the basic facts and features of the major celestial bodies within the solar system. This provided a core body of knowledge for them to develop their projects on.

The section on each of the planets also includes details for some of the space missions to the celestial body. The movies that are presented in the application include:

- Size comparison
- Earth's cycles
- Solar eclipse
- The moon's phases

The students also developed an understanding of the vast distances involved in space exploration and the potential issues this raised for sustainable return space travel.

Our World and Our Choice: Physical Sciences at a Glance

Al Gore's electronic book, Our Choice, is used as a core resource for this multidiscipline science unit. The focus of the unit is the environment and conservation of energy and resources. Students develop an understanding of the issues and concepts by looking at various chapters of the ebook.

McREL Science—Earth & Space Sciences Standards at a Glance
Level 3 (Grades 6–8)

Understands the composition and structure of the universe and the Earth's place in it

1. Knows characteristics and movement patterns of the planets in our Solar System (e.g., planets differ in size, composition, and surface features; planets move around the Sun in elliptical orbits; some planets have moons, rings of particles, and other satellites orbiting them).

2. Knows how the regular and predictable motions of the Earth and Moon explain phenomena on Earth (e.g., the day, the year, phases of the Moon, eclipses, tides, shadows).

3. Knows characteristics of the Sun and its position in the universe (e.g., the Sun is a medium-sized star; it is the closest star to Earth; it is the central and largest body in the Solar System; it is located at the edge of a disk-shaped galaxy).

4. Knows characteristics and movement patterns of asteroids, comets, and meteors.

5. Knows characteristics and movement patterns of asteroids, comets, and meteors.

6. Knows that the universe consists of many billions of galaxies (each containing many billions of stars) and that incomprehensible distances (measured in light years) separate these galaxies and stars from one another and from the Earth.

7. Knows that the Earth is distinguished from other known celestial bodies in that it is the only planet known to harbor life, although similar planets might yet be discovered in the universe.

The research starts with Chapter 1— "What Goes Up Must Come Down." This chapter sets the scene of energy use and some of the potential consequences for uncontrolled use or overuse of various energy sources (figure 5.9). The students read through the chapter and take notes using either iThoughtsHD or Pages, depending on their preference. They manipulate the interactive infographics on global warming and pollutants and watch the animations on greenhouse gases, smog, and pollution.

Figure 5.9—Al Gore's "Our World, Our Choice"

Describe, Analyze, and Evaluate

Once the students have completed the research element, they are then handed their first independent learning task. Using the desktop publishing templates in Pages (figure 5.10), the students are to prepare and present a four-color poster that describes, analyzes, and evaluates a single aspect of the effects of pollution.

Figure 5.10—iWorks Pages has a selection of templates the students can use. In this case, they selected the poster as the template to develop their "effects of pollution" poster.

The task is scaffolded to support the students in developing a suitable product. The three different cognitive tasks are clearly explained to them so they can address each with accuracy. They are, in brief:

- **Description**—This is asking the four basic questions about their chosen aspect: What, Where, When, and Who.

- **Analysis**—This is asking the How and Why questions: How did this happen, and Why did it happen? Break the issue down into its component parts.

- **Evaluation**—What are the impacts, importance, effectiveness, and relationships affected by this? Make a judgement based on the analysis and description.

Graphic Design

The students are told that the purpose of the poster is to investigate a single aspect of pollution and that their target audience is their peers. When the students work on the poster, they are asked to constantly reflect on the two core questions that underpin graphical design and presentation:

- Is it suitable for the **audience**?

- Is it suitable for the **purpose**?

During the unit, the students develop an understanding of the importance of energy to organisms, as well as understanding that energy cannot be created or destroyed (the law of conservation of energy). The second task for the unit requires the students to synthesize information from various chapters into a short advertisement using still images, text, and narration. This part of the project is developed using iMovie (figure 5.11).

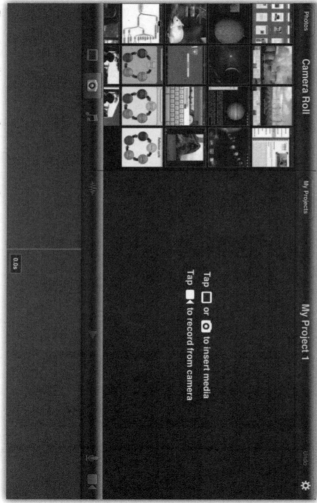

Figure 5.11—iMovie page for inserting media

The task was for the students to consider the information presented within the ebook and adapt it to suit their households and local environments. They were required to produce a 30-second advertisement on how to save and conserve energy. To make the task manageable, several restrictions were added. These included:

- Maximum of 30-second duration
- Only use still images they have recorded
- Use iMovie as the tool to construct the final product

Students could also use the Animoto application to create the short video.

Working in small groups, the students were first required to discover background information about how they could conserve energy or minimize waste within their own households. This was a brainstorm where the students jotted down all their ideas, no matter how wacky they may have seemed. The students then refined the list down to three to four ideas that were feasible and manageable. From this short list, they selected one or two ideas that they could present in the 30-second advertisement.

The second part of the background was investigating what they could do using iMovie. Having refined the ideas down, the students then created their solution. Here they outlined the concept to present to the teacher either as a short paragraph or in bullet points. Some students did this in Notes, others in Pages, and some used pen and paper.

In the design phase, they storyboarded how they thought their advertisement would run and the script they would use. Some students considered camera angles, transitions, and animations that suited the purpose of the video and the audience they were presenting to. From there, the students used the camera on the iPad to take the required images. These were then imported into iMovie. Some students added the images directly into iMovie by clicking on the Record Media button. Once the media was added, the students adjusted the timeline to set the duration of the imported images. They then added narration and, in some cases, also created backing music in Garageband, while others created loops using the built-in sample music.

The product was saved and sent to the camera roll and displayed using the VGA adaptor on the projector. An email version of the product was sent to the teacher.

McREL Science—Physical Sciences Standards at a Glance
Level 3 (Grades 6–8) Standard 8

Understands the sources and properties of energy

2. Understands the law of conservation of energy (i.e., energy cannot be created or destroyed but only changed from one form to another).

4. Knows how the Sun acts as a major source of energy for changes on the Earth's surface (i.e., the Sun loses energy by emitting light; some of this light is transferred to the Earth in a range of wavelengths including visible light, infrared radiation, and ultraviolet radiation).

11. Understands the origins and environmental impacts of renewable and nonrenewable resources, including energy sources like fossil fuels (e.g., coal, oil, natural gas).

McREL Science—Life Sciences Standards at a Glance

Level 3 (Grades 6–8) Standard 6

Understands the relationship among organisms and their physical environment

4. Knows how energy is transferred through food webs in an ecosystem (e.g., energy enters ecosystems as sunlight, and green plants transfer this energy into chemical energy through photosynthesis; this chemical energy is passed from organism to organism; animals get energy from oxidizing their food, releasing some of this energy as heat).

Summary

Science is a core knowledge area. The teaching of science is a powerful mixture of key knowledge, understanding, and hands-on activities and learning, whether learning to respect and protect animals and the environment or challenging our understanding of space travel and the world we live in.

The applications selected are some of the best of their type that are available. Reference applications, such as SolarWalk and NASA, provide detailed resources for the students to base their learning on and to synthesize practical knowledge from. The applications, such as Rat Dissection and Frog Dissection, allow the students to develop an understanding of functional anatomy in a suitable and acceptable mode. Unlike a physical dissection, the simulation allows the students to repeat the task any number of times, either as a rehearsal for the real dissections or as a replacement for it, or just to further their understanding.

Al Gore's Our Choice challenges us in a number of ways. It encourages us to examine our behaviors and actions and shows us a different pathway forward to a more sustainable world. It also makes us rethink what a book can be and shows us the future direction of publishing. The challenges presented in this unit of work bring together publishing and the principles of graphical design with the core science curriculum.

Tools for Science: Apps in the Spotlight

Name: Adobe Photoshop Express

Cost: Free with purchased extension packs

iTunes URL: http://bit.ly/N6Os6Y

Type: Image and photo editor (simple)

Device: iPad / iPod Touch / iPhone

Description: This is a simple free image and photo editor that allows the user to manipulate and crop images and adjust color, contrast, saturation, and so on. This tool is more adaptable and useful than the built-in features in the photo container in iOS 5.

Name: Al Gore—Our Choice: A Plan to Solve the Climate Crisis

Cost: $4.99

iTunes URL: http://bit.ly/PGQGlF

Type: Reference application

Device: iPad / iPhone

Description: This is a benchmark application for how electronic books should be. The book is easy to navigate using gestures to move quickly between chapters and pages. The product contains interactive animations and infographics as well as image and documentary footage. At various points are short audio snippets by Al Gore explaining the various elements and sections. The images link through to maps showing the location of the different pictures and clips.

Name: iMovie

Cost: $4.99

iTunes URL: http://bit.ly/OKSkOi

Type: Video editor

Device: iPad / iPhone

Description: This is a powerful video editor that allows users to record images and video directly into the timeline as well as import media from the camera roll or from folders in Photos. Sound effects and tracks are available within the program to enhance the product. The product comes with eight different themes, each with its own titles, transitions, and background music that can be used, or more experienced users can develop their own to suit the task and the audience. The product can be shared either by playing it on or from the iPad or by sharing via email or YouTube.

Name: iThoughtsHD

Cost: $9.99

iTunes URL: http://bit.ly/N2xDMr

Type: Mind mapping and graphical organizer

Device: iPad

Description: A powerful and flexible mind mapping tool that allows users to quickly construct mind maps of concepts and ideas. Insert images directly from the camera or from the photos container on your iPad. iThoughtsHD exports into a variety of mind mapping formats, allowing students to collaborate and share with their peers and teachers independent of them having this specific product. Students are able to link different concepts to show the relationship between core ideas and can easily insert images into the nodes.

Name: iWorks Pages

Cost: $9.99

iTunes URL: http://bit.ly/RkOB6M

Type: Word processor and simple desktop publishing application

Device: iPad / iPhone

Description: iWorks Pages is a straightforward and simple word processor. It has all of the basic functions expected of a simple word processor or basic desktop publishing tool. Images, graphs, tables, and charts can be easily added and a variety of different styles and templates are easily accessible. Documents can be uploaded and downloaded from iCloud. Students can submit their documents in a variety of formats including .doc and .pdf.

Name: NASA App

Cost: Free

iTunes URL: http://bit.ly/MgsoV5

Type: Reference and news application

Device: iPad / iPod Touch / iPhone

Description: A free application from NASA, the National Aeronautics and Space Administration, this tool provides a dynamic reference and news tool for the students. With detailed but child-friendly information, this is an excellent reference tool allowing students to research characteristics and movement patterns of the planets and other celestial bodies. Discover information about the sun and other stars, as well as inquire about current and past space missions.

Name: Rat Dissection

Cost: $3.99

iTunes URL: http://bit.ly/OEOrag

Type: Simulation and reference

Device: iPad

Description: The Rat Dissection app is the second dissection simulation application developed by Emantras, with the first being Frog Dissection. This tool allows students to simulate the dissection of a rat and examine the internal anatomy using the 3D anatomy view. Using this app, students are able to quickly develop an understanding of the core components of the respiratory, digestive, and excretory systems of mammals. Clicking on the different organs will access information about that organ or system. Students can find information on the digestive, respiratory, cardio-vascular, and excretory systems.

Name: Solar Walk

Cost: $2.99

iTunes URL: http://bit.ly/N6QIv9

Type: Reference application

Device: iPad / iPod Touch / iPhone

Description: Solar Walk is a reference application for the solar system, with limited simulation features allowing students to "fly to a planet." This application provides an extensive body of knowledge about the solar system as well as movies and interactive elements. The 3D feature requires the user to have the 3D glasses. The true-to-scale tool allows students to gain a perspective of the relative size of the different celestial bodies. A useful component of the application is a screen capture tool allowing students to use the images they capture within the program for presentations.

Name: VoiceThread

Cost: Free (requires a VoiceThread account)

iTunes URL: http://bit.ly/NWXN25

Type: Presentation—audio and visual

Device: iPad / iPod Touch / iPhone

Description: VoiceThread allows students to create a "voicethread" from their iPad. VoiceThread is a slideshow-style presentation tool that enables users to add images and text, as well as narrate their presentations. Once online, peers and teachers can be invited to leave voice comments and feedback. This creates a threaded discussion based around spoken comments rather than the usual text-based posts. Using the VoiceThread application on the iPad allows students to create presentations using the images from their camera and photos container on the iPad. VoiceThread helps students who would normally struggle with public speaking to create and narrate presentations of high quality.

Chapter 6

Tools for ESOL

Tools for ESOL

This chapter explores how applications are used to develop the language acquisition and skills of students for whom English is a second language. The applications selected will support the student's learning of spoken and written language. With the written language, these applications will support the development of grammar, spelling, and sentence structure. The chapter primarily focuses on English as a second language, but many of the applications could also be used in learning other languages. However, the focus here is acquiring and developing skills in English. The applications selected and detailed here are Play2Learn, SpellBoard, iTranslate, and Sentence Builder.

Setting the Scene

Maho is a 14-year-old Japanese student participating in an English language exchange for six months. With a grasp of simple conversational English and basic written vocabulary, she is placed with an English-speaking family for six months. This full immersion English language experience will assist her in both her understanding and her development of spoken and written English skills.

Maho has been provided with an iPad as a personal learning device and has access to a range of applications, such as Play2Learn, that will assist her in reaching her goal of improved fluency in spoken and written English (figure 6.1).

Figure 6.1— With Play2Learn, Maho is learning the spoken and written form of common animals. By clicking on the sheep image, the written form of the noun is displayed and then she can listen to the spoken word.

Developing Vocabulary

To develop her oral and written vocabulary, Maho uses the graphical Play2Learn application for English. The application has a wide range of thematic palettes that examine related vocabulary themes.

Play2Learn has both a testing and learning mode. In the testing and learning mode, clicking on the image will show the written word and play its correct pronunciation in a sound bite. In the testing mode, the application randomly selects a term from the palette and pronounces it, and then the student has to select the corresponding image.

The application allows Maho to learn the spoken and written terms and then test herself by listening to the spoken word and selecting it from the array of images. Maho receives instant feedback in the testing mode as correct answers are applauded and incorrect responses are marked by the sound of breaking glass (figure 6.2).

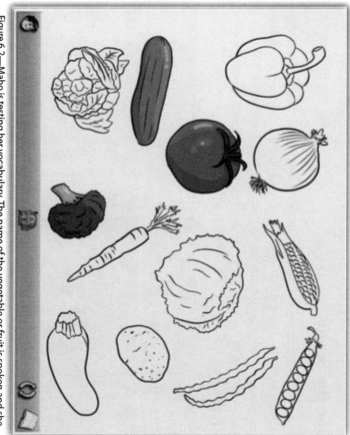

Figure 6.2—Maho is testing her vocabulary. The name of the vegetable or fruit is spoken and she has to click on the corresponding image.

Maho's teacher uses the application for self-directed learning and encourages her to practice the vocabulary regularly. As part of the immersion program, Maho, her host family, and her fellow exchange students often participate in group activities and programs. One of the activities is a visit to a local farm.

Maho's teacher will prepare her and her fellow exchange students by setting class and homework activities that involve learning the vocabulary associated with the visit—in this case, the animals and vegetables that she may encounter on her visit. Reinforcement with practical exercises like the visits and activities help Maho to further develop her language skills.

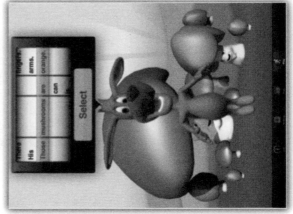

Figure 6.3— Themed palettes in Play2Learn

The themed palettes (figure 6.3) cover common vocabulary, and some of the palettes are extension packs that need to be purchased separately. They include:

- The body, limbs, and face
- The family
- Transportation and vehicles
- Colors and shapes
- Clothing
- Food, including fruit and vegetables, party foods, place settings, etc.
- Animals—insects and bugs, domestic, and zoo
- Landscapes and scenery
- The house, including the bedroom, bathroom, kitchen, and exterior
- Computers, sports, tools, toys, and more

With the extension packs purchased and installed, Maho has more than twenty vocabulary palettes to choose from. The spoken and written elements assist her as she develops her vocabulary, pronunciation, and written expression.

The Play2Learn applications are available in a number of different languages. While detailed here for a student learning English, the languages that are available include French, German, Spanish, Italian, Polish, and more. All the applications have a common theme and structure, making them good standard vocabulary tools for language acquisition and reinforcement.

Developing Sentence Structure

To further develop and support Maho in her understanding of sentence structure, she is encouraged to use the Sentence Builder application. This tool takes her through the construction of simple sentences (figure 6.4) and provides immediate feedback. Like Play2Learn, this app uses both written and auditory cues to provide a multisensory approach. The application requires the learner to assemble a sentence from the range of words available. The student will select suitable modifiers, adjectives, and verbs with increasing complexity as he or she progresses through the learning journey. The application will read the correct sentence out loud, supporting the student's oral language skills as well as the construction of written text.

Figure 6.4—Building sentences in Sentence Builder

The application comes with a simple younger person module, but can be expanded to include the teen boy and teen girl modules. These provide a progression from simple sentences to more complicated ones.

Within each module, the application presents images as the stimulus for the sentence. The images range from cartoon figures to pictures of young adults, depending on which module is selected. The learner then constructs the sentence by selecting the correct words from the range available on the rollers. The number of wheels on the selector increases with the complexity of the sentence.

Maho listens to the instructions and then makes a sentence about the picture. She manipulates the rollers to construct the sentence and clicks on Select when she is ready. The application then provides immediate feedback, and she either proceeds to the next sentence or continues to rebuild the sentence until she achieves success.

Maho progresses through the three levels of complexity, and she is able to access the statistics to see her success at the different levels. The program initially focuses on the connector words and the construction of grammatically correct sentences. At the simplest level, the sentences are only three to four words long, but as Maho progresses, the complexity of the sentences increases.

In the first level, the student chooses the modifier and the verb in each sentence. At the second level, the modifier, adjective, and verb are chosen. On the third and final level, the student picks the modifier, verb, and adjective from a selection of five choices per picker.

Translating Back and Forth

When presented with a written phrase in English that she does not understand, Maho is encouraged to use the iTranslate application. This tool allows her to translate backward and forward between a wide range of languages, including English and Japanese (figure 6.5).

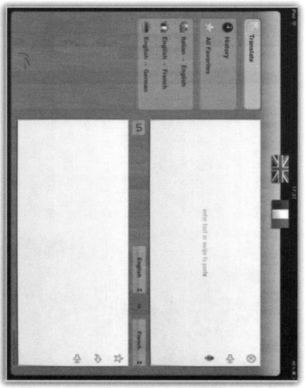

Figure 6.5—iTranslate works across a broad range of international dialects

Typing or pasting a phrase into the English box quickly shows a written translation in the Japanese box. Maho is encouraged to use the Switch function to ensure that the translation she has created is accurate in translating in both directions. She also uses this application to help her in constructing sentences.

Using the text-to-speech option allows Maho to listen to a translated phrase and see it in written format. Maho made use of text-to-speech in English and Japanese, but this feature is available in a number of languages, including German, French, Spanish, Korean, and more.

Voice recognition was another tool that Maho used, which is a purchased add-on. She spoke into the iPad's microphone and was able to see her spoken words translated into the language of choice. This can be affected by accents, pronunciation, and the clarity of the speaker's voice. The spoken version of the translation is another useful tool for Maho to learn the oral, as well as written, aspects of English.

This is a powerful learning tool that can be used to enable communication at its simplest level and as a tool for the language learner to construct and deconstruct written and spoken language. The application is not without limitations and does provide a literal translation that often misses the subtleties of the language. The product does come with a dictionary that allows the language learner to delve deeper into the meaning of the text and to consider alternatives.

Developing Spelling

Spelling is a critical aspect of written language. SpellBoard is an application that is used to support Maho as she develops her written English. It allows her to test and reinforce the spelling of simple English words.

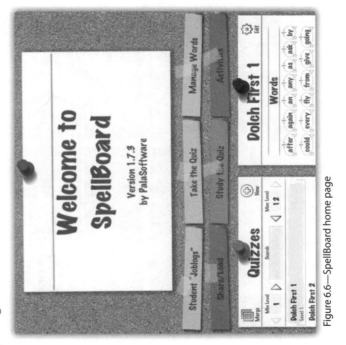

Figure 6.6—SpellBoard home page

The application has a large number of preconstructed spelling lists at various levels of difficulty. The learner selects a list, and then either studies the quiz by clicking on the Study the Quiz button or tests him- or herself by selecting Take the Quiz (figure 6.6).

Testing involves listening to a phrase containing the focus word, and then seeing the sentence without the focus word. Maho then has to add the focus word and spell it correctly. The use of spoken phrases in the testing element supports her acquisition of oral language.

In this example (figure 6.7), the focus word is "where." Maho listens to the spoken phrase "where are you" and then, using the scratch pad, writes out the spelling of the word. Once she is happy with the spelling, she types the correct answer into the text field. The use of the scratch pad is optional; students can enter the word immediately into the text field.

Figure 6.7—SpellBoard quiz using the scratch pad

The application has different levels of complexity and difficulty to continue to challenge students as they progress in their learning journey. The application includes a library containing multiple tests of differing levels of complexity, providing a suitable learning progression from simple to advanced, aiding the student in both written and oral language skills.

An exciting feature for both students and teachers is the ability to develop tests. The developer selects the words to be tested and constructs a sentence in written and spoken form. The application records the phrase and the focus word, and then adds the completed elements to a spelling test.

This has positive outcomes for both students and teachers. For students, they are able to take a degree of ownership of their learning. By working through this process, they are developing a far greater depth of understanding, not only of correct spelling, but also sentence structure and oral pronunciation of the term and phrase. For teachers, it allows them to develop tests that are specific to the activity or tasks the students are undertaking at the time. An example of this would be a spelling test as reinforcement for the terms the students have learned on their trip to the farm.

The application is available in four different languages: English, French, German, and Spanish. However, the ease of developing your own tests means that this is a tool that can be used in many languages. Teachers and their students can construct spelling tests in their language of choice, recording their spoken phrase, entering the written form of the phrase, and identifying the focus word being tested.

Summary

Learning a second language is challenging, but the advantages of such an undertaking are huge. Using applications that are fun and engaging makes the task less of a job and more of a game. Students should be encouraged to use these tools to reinforce their learning and to develop their own learning resources that they can share with their peers. A tool such as SpellBoard goes beyond the primary role of supporting the development of spelling, and it allows students to develop their own tests. Incorporating spoken and written language are powerful tools in the teaching toolkit. This empowers students and allows them to take ownership of their learning.

iTranslate provides a fast and straightforward medium to assist students in translating and understanding other languages. The ability to switch the translation back and forth provides them with a quick means for checking accuracy. This application supports a number of different languages and allows students to switch quickly between their mother tongue and English.

The Play2Learn apps have a range of language vocabulary tools that provide a consistent and diverse range of palettes of everyday items. This tool allows students to learn and test themselves, providing immediate feedback using the testing tool built into each template. When used in conjunction with class activities, this tool helps students to develop and reinforce vocabulary.

Sentence Builder is a powerful grammatical tool for learning English, whether as a second language learner or as a student of English. The differing levels of complexity and age sets means that students across a wide age spectrum will be challenged and supported by this application.

Other Applications Worth Considering

Japanese Phrases—Free

http://bit.ly/lN2AbKk

As the name suggests, this is the free version of Japanese Phrases. This application comes with advertisements in the free version; for a small cost, these can be removed. The upgrade to the full version is more expensive but adds a great deal to the application.

This application gives students access to study cards that link audio and written material, lessons, and quizzes that assist in learning Japanese.

Comic Life

http://bit.ly/lMC6g95

Comic Life is a purchased application that can be used in any number of teaching and learning situations. However, for the language learner it is a powerful tool that allows them to construct comics from single page to multipage, and annotate these with speech bubbles, callouts, and captions. While Comic Life is only available in English, the keyboard on the iPad does allow you to add accents by holding down a letter key, and after a few moments the accent options appear (figure 6.8). Students are able to construct visual stories and present these with the correct inflection and accents, rather than ignoring these important elements of language.

Figure 6.8—Accessing accents in Comic Life

Sock Puppets

http://bit.ly/OEPabA

This application allows the user to create sock puppet- and cartoon-themed short video clips (figure 6.9). The initial clips are limited to thirty seconds, but can be extended to ninety seconds with the help of an in-application purchase. You can select the number of characters or puppets (you assign a voice to each character as you speak by clicking on the puppet to be animated), the background, and props and scenery. Each participant speaks his or her lines, and then clicks on the next speaker's character to animate the other puppet. The completed video can be shared via Facebook or YouTube in the basic version, but can be rendered and saved to the photos container if the extension is purchased. The application is fun and engaging, and it allows students to develop their conversational language skills in a captivating and creative setting.

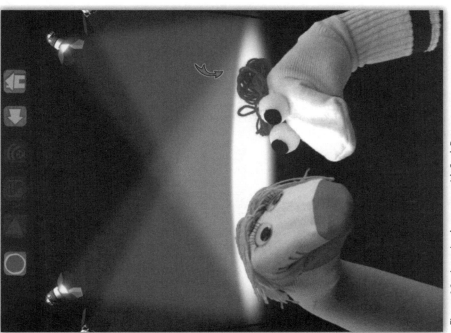

Figure 6.9—Learning language with Sock Puppets

Tools for ESOL: Apps in the Spotlight

Name: iTranslate

Cost: Free

iTunes URL: http://bit.ly/N6ROXN

Type: Translation tool requiring Internet connectivity

Device: iPad / iPod Touch / iPhone

Description: This is a free translation tool that is available for the iPad, iPhone, and the iPod Touch. The application supports translations between multiple languages. The voice translation and playback are powerful tools that reinforce language aquisition. Extension packs are available for purchase for making the translation ad-free or for voice recognition. Voice recognition is available for English, Spanish, French, Japanese, German, and Italian.

Name: Play2Learn English

Cost: $1.99

iTunes URL: http://bit.ly/OMQGu0

Type: Oral and written vocabulary development tool in a range of languages

Device: iPad

Description: This is a graphical oral language vocabulary tool. Students click on the themed palette to select it, and then learn the vocabulary by repetition and by testing themselves in testing mode. The written form of the word is available by hovering over the cartoon-style image. This application is available in a wide range of languages and has a number of extensions that contain even more themes. The language packs will cover much of the basic nouns required for day-to-day activities and conversations. Extension packs are available for purchase through the application.

Name: Sentence Builder

Cost: $3.99

iTunes URL: http://bit.ly/NOyQZh

Type: English language sentence construction tool

Device: iPad / iPod Touch / iPhone

Description: This is a graphical sentence construction tool. There are three levels of complexity within each pack, and themed extension packages suitable to older students. The tool requires students to assemble a sentence by selecting the modifier, verb, and adjective. Statistics of success and attempts are available for each learner. The learners are required to sign in to the account and the application records data to provide simple learning analytics. This application is only available in English. It is a very useful and applicable tool for ESL learners as well as in the language arts classroom. Extension packs are available for purchase through the application, and are for teenage girls and boys.

Name: SpellBoard

Cost: $4.99

iTunes URL: http://bit.ly/PqySkM

Type: Spelling drill tool available in four languages, with written and oral component

Device: iPad

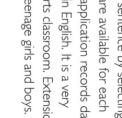

Description: This is a spelling development tool that comes with a number of basic tests of various levels of difficulty. The tests are based around a spoken sentence with emphasis on the target word. The test's content is easily editable. Teachers can record and develop their own sentences and tests, making it an adaptable and flexible tool for reinforcing and developing spelling skills. Students can create their own spelling tests, particularly when they are learning a second language. This application is available in four languages: English, French, German, and Spanish.

Chapter **7**

Tools for **Speaking in Tongues**

7 Tools for Speaking in Tongues

Maureen is a French language teacher who works in conjunction with Gilbert, the oral language teacher, to deliver the middle school French language course. The course itself has two components—the written aspect and the oral or spoken component. Each is equally important for the holistic development and understanding of the French language.

Understanding Culture and Exploring Using Google Earth and Keynote

For Maureen, a teacher of written French, the culture is almost as important as the recognition, understanding, and construction of the written language. While in the later years at school, students may have the opportunity to travel to a French-speaking country to immerse themselves in the language and culture, this is not available to the middle school students. To gain some understanding of French culture, the students must explore the history of France and its places of historical significance. Maureen uses Google Earth's satellite and hybrid views to provide a street-level perspective of Paris and its iconic landmarks (figure 7.1).

Figure 7.1—The different map views or layers can be accessed by the layers menu in the top left-hand corner of the application. You can select whether you want different layers switched on or off. The application allows students to link to Wikipedia to research the background of the historical site.

The students are investigating some of the famous landmarks of Paris and their historical significance. Maureen asked the students what they knew about Paris, and they were able to list a number of significant sites, one of which was the Arc de Triomphe. This monument, which honors those who died in the French Revolution, stands in the centre of the Place Charles de Gaulle at the end of the Champs-Élysées. The Arc de Triomphe, or in its English translation, the Triumphal Arch, is of huge historical importance to the French culture.

While the overhead perspective is useful, the students prefer using the tilt perspective to gain a different view (figure 7.2). They are able to tilt the view by sliding two fingers up and down the iPad's screen to change the angle of view. Clicking on the image icons visible at the top of the screen displays images taken from this point.

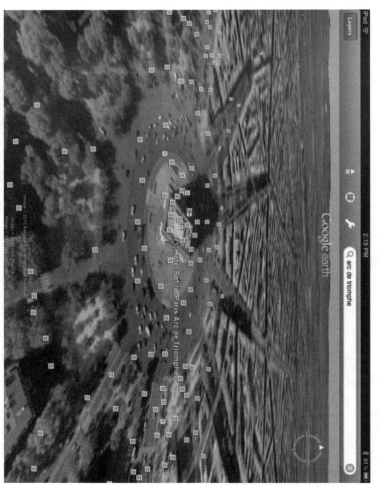

Figure 7.2—The Arc de Triomphe viewed from a different perspective. The image icons on the page are geo-tagged images taken approximately from that position. Access to these images provides the students with a unique view of the Arc.

The students are then asked to prepare a brief presentation to the class about the landmark they have researched using Keynote. The assignment was in two parts, the first of which was to describe the landmark. They asked the Who, What, Where, and When questions. Then they were asked to explain why they thought the landmark was significant and how it was significant. The students were asked to provide a variety of different visual perspectives that would be captivating and interesting for their peers.

The students linked their iPads to the projectors using a VGA adaptor. As they were developing their presentations, the students added key notes and information to the presenter's notes (figure 7.3).

Figure 7.3—Adding presenter's notes in Keynote

When the students presented their reports, they saw the slides projected and their notes appeared on the device. As the students progress through the course, their vocabulary expands. However, both written and oral vocabulary require reinforcement to maintain and develop. Gilbert and Maureen use a number of different tools to reinforce this progression.

Summary

Using Google Earth as a visualization tool, in addition to the experiences and culture that the teacher brings to the class, allows students to develop an understanding of some of the aspects of French culture. The students' learning is reinforced by the development of a presentation requiring them to verbalize and visualize the significant landmarks. They describe (who, what, where, and when) their selected site and then explain (how and why) it is significant to French culture. In the example of the Arc de Triomphe, they must explore one of the cornerstones that built modern France—the French Revolution.

Teaching Vocabulary Using Play2Learn

One of the first tools students use as they begin their learning journey of a second language is Play2Learn French, an oral and written vocabulary tool (figure 7.4). Play2Learn is available in a range of languages, including English, to support language acquisition in a variety of different tongues.

The application comes with a basic vocabulary pack that can be expanded with extension packs. The vocabulary is arranged into a series of palettes based around a theme. The themes cover a wide range of common vocabulary elements. Each palette has two modes presented in a simple cartoon-style format:

- Learning and repetition
- Testing and feedback

Fig 7.4—Play2Learn French in action. Students click on an image to hear it spoken in the language.

In the learning and repetition mode, the student clicks on the different elements of the image and listens to the spoken noun, and then reads the written form of the word. The palettes cover a wide range of themes, and the spoken language is clear and recorded in the voice of a native speaker. Students can repeat the sound bite as often as required to enable them to assimilate and replicate the pronunciation. The written form of the noun aids the development of written language skills.

In the testing option, the application randomly selects the spoken phrase. The student clicks on the appropriate image and is rewarded either by applause or by the sound of breaking glass, depending on the success or failure of the selection. There is no scoring mechanism showing success or failure rates, so the test is nonthreatening. Students will often spend long periods of their own time testing themselves to gain mastery of each palette of terms.

Play2Learn French is a useful tool for both Maureen and Gilbert as it links written and spoken vocabulary. The clear pronunciation and spelling of many common terms allows students to practice their vocabulary in an entertaining and engaging way. This tool is not limited to just French; it is available in a number of different languages including English (see the ESOL chapter for how this is used for English second language students), Spanish (Castellano and Latin American), German, Mandarin Chinese, Russian, and Portuguese (European and Brazilian).

In testing mode (figure 7.5), the student listens to the spoken word or term, and then clicks on the appropriate image that represents the spoken noun. Success is greeted by applause and an inaccurate selection by the sound of breaking glass. It is recommended that students use headphones for this, as the noise of several iPads running this program can make hearing the spoken words difficult.

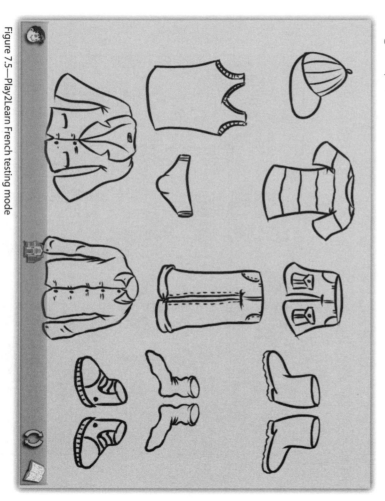

Figure 7.5—Play2Learn French testing mode

Say It with Pictures Using Comic Life

Another tool that Maureen uses with her classes is Plasq's Comic Life. Comic Life allows students to develop comic strips or cartoons from a number of different templates and styles. Maureen uses Comic Life for vocabulary and written language development.

The students are able to insert images of common items (figure 7.6) and then add speech or text bubbles or callouts to suitably label the images. This tool is used to reinforce the vocabulary learned during the school day. Comics are particularly useful in developing conversational language.

The speech and thought bubbles are used to present the conversational language, while the caption boxes are used for formal text, which sets the scene or indicates action.

As the students progress in the development of their language, they can use the Comic Life app to tell short stories using conversational language. They can use the cameras built into the iPad to take staged pictures and then add them to the placeholders. Often the students will create these from a new blank page, adding the number of placeholders they require and resizing these to suit their needs (figure 7.7). They will rotate them to add variety to the layout and are able to place the containers anywhere on the page.

Figure 7.6—Play2Learn French testing mode

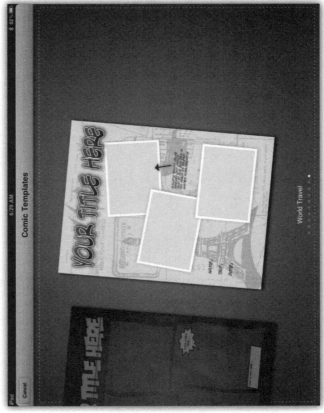

Figure 7.7—Adding placeholders for images in Comic Life

As their confidence grows, so do their stories. They will start to create multipage comics, adding in shapes like arrows, circles, squares, diamonds, and more.

Though the stories start simple, students quickly progress to more complex themes and conversations. They find the combination of visual images and text engaging and enjoyable, and the interface is simple and easy to use.

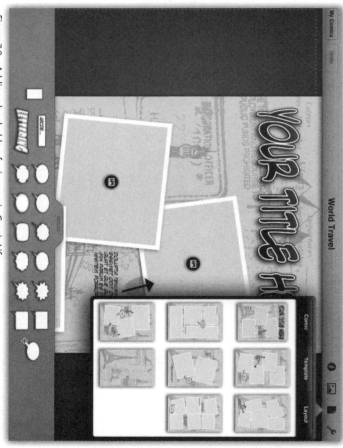

Figure 7.8—Adding placeholders for images in Comic Life

Students are not limited to single-page products, but can add multiple pages in a variety of formats (figure 7.8). This allows students to create graphical novels as they grow in confidence and ability. They are also able to manipulate the layouts to create their own structure to suit their needs.

The students share their work by either printing it directly from the iPad to a connected printer or by emailing their comic as an image file or a PDF document (figure 7.9).

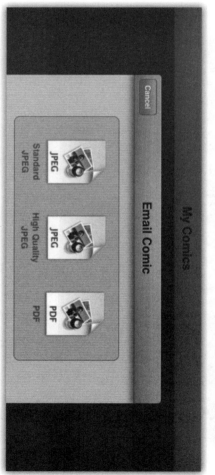

Figure 7.9—Emailing comics in different image formats

The use of comics and cartoons is engaging for students. It provides a degree of relevance, as they are creating their own products and stories in an engaging and enjoyable manner. In addition, it helps to develop their oral and written literacy as they construct both conversational and formal prose.

Introducing a New Tool—Three and No Repeats

While Maureen is a capable user of the iPad, she does not profess to be an expert. When she is introducing a new software tool to the students, she does not need to know all of the tricks and techniques, because she is going to allow her students to discover these and present them back to the class.

The iPad 2 allows full-screen mirroring. When connected to the projector or monitor, a student can demonstrate the technique or trick on the iPad, and it is easily seen by the rest of the class. (In the first version of the iPad, applications like Projector! would have been needed to do this, and even then this only worked with some applications). The method that Maureen uses is called "Three and No Repeats."

Maureen introduces the application to the class and explains the basic functions and outcomes that she wants from the use of the tool. In the case of Comic Life, Maureen wanted the students to be able to produce engaging documents that reinforced the vocabulary they were learning. Then she explained the rules of Three and No Repeats:

- Every student will be presenting one technique or trick to the class.

- The students are to find three tricks or techniques that they can demonstrate to the class within a 5–10 minute time frame. The reason for the students finding three techniques is No Repeats.

- No Repeats means just that—the students have to show a new trick or technique each time.

The presentations are very quick as the students rapidly come forward to the connected iPad and show their discoveries. One student may show the class how to change the background color on the page, another may show how to insert a texture or image, another how to print, and another how to add a speech bubble.

The outcome of this approach is that Maureen has scaffolded a learning experience for the students. They have explored and discovered the application for themselves, shifting the emphasis of learning from the teacher to the students. They have discovered the approach and have greater ownership of the learning. The students also become each other's first port of call in the class for support and assistance when they need to do something with this application.

Maureen selects who starts the presentations. She will usually ask the student or students who have been struggling the most to come up first. This way, there is no chance that the technique has been previously demonstrated. The most capable students are left until the end and they quickly adapt and change their presentations as the concepts, ideas, and processes they have discovered are presented. This approach means that all the students are successful and the most able are challenged and engaged throughout the class.

Bringing Spelling and Speaking Together with SpellBoard and iTranslate

SpellBoard is a spelling reinforcement tool. It is used in the acquisition and reinforcement of spelling in English language classrooms. SpellBoard enables teachers to assist students in developing their own spelling and oral language tests (figure 7.10).

Figure 7.10—SpellBoard can develop custom tests to suit the learner

The process is straightforward. The teacher decides on a list of words that the students need to learn. The students add these words to a new test. They record the spoken word using the built-in microphone. Then the students enter the word into a phrase or short sentence and record the whole phrase. This provides context as well as reinforcement of oral language skills. The students repeat this process until the word list has been completed. They then try out the newly created tests on their peers. The teacher is able to circulate around the room, correcting minor errors and improving the pronunciation of the term and spoken phrase. The students can share their tests with the teacher (figure 7.11). The options for this include:

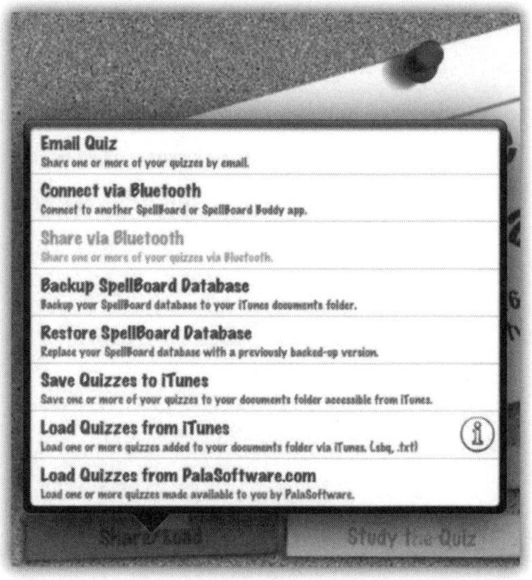

- emailing the quiz
- connecting and sharing via Bluetooth
- loading and saving spelling and vocabulary lists from iTunes

Figure 7.11—Menu for sharing options in SpellBoard

This tool is created by the same company that produces Mathboard, a mathematics learning tool. It is good for reinforcing the underlying concepts of spelling, and since the phrase is spoken as well as presented visually, it also strengthens the link between the spoken and written forms of the words.

iTranslate as a Reference Tool

Students can use iTranslate to check and proof their phrases. They can copy their spoken phrase and paste it into iTranslate (figure 7.12). This application allows them to translate written language into a variety of different tongues. In some languages, they can also listen to a spoken translation.

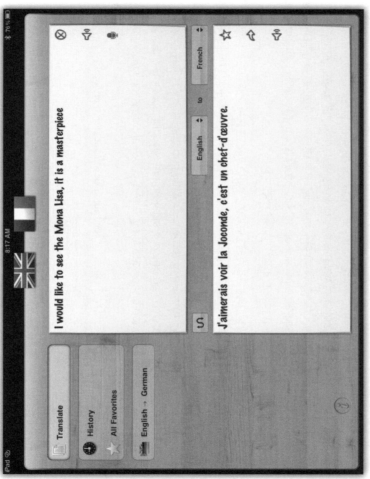

Figure 7.12—Paste a phrase into iTranslate and choose your language

Much like using the "Three and No Repeats" technique, this process shifts the ownership of the learning process to the student. The students are constructing their learning, and this frees the teacher to provide immediate feedback and support.

Conversations Across and Beyond the Classroom with Skype and FaceTime

Gilbert, the oral language teacher, uses voice and video conferencing tools to support the acquisition and reinforcement of oral language. Using FaceTime and Skype, students can conduct spoken conversations with their teacher or their peers. Using the Skype Education Network, the class is able to stretch beyond the four walls of the classroom and make contact with students around the world.

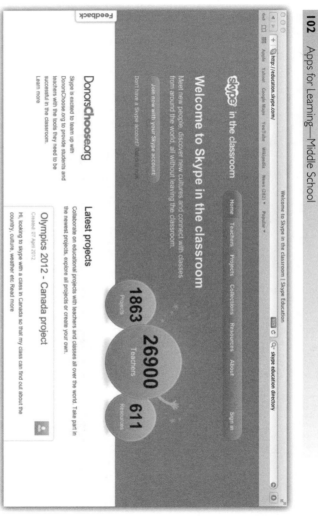

Figure 7.13—The Skype Education Network home page

The Skype Education Network (figure 7.13) provides a powerful set of resources and an extensive directory of teachers and projects that can be accessed by teachers anywhere in the world. The Skype Education Network is accessible at http://education.skype.com.

Gilbert initially has the students working in pairs using Skype. The students use the video from the iPad camera and earphone/microphone headsets to reduce the level of noise in the classroom. They also add to the conversation using the instant messaging feature.

Gilbert set strict guidelines and rules regarding the use of the tools, and moves around the classroom working with the students. Since the learning objective is speaking and chatting in French, the students are only allowed to speak in French. The students often have a list of "stock phrases" they have rehearsed and are able to use in these simple starting conversations. This process of short conversations, the use of stock phrases, and the separation that the use of technology allows within a classroom enhances the learning experiences of the students.

Once the students have developed a degree of confidence and basic competence, it is time to reach beyond the classroom. Students learn a language because they wish to apply it and use it in the real world. To facilitate this end goal, Gilbert has established contact with schools around the world. In collaboration with the teachers and students in the distant schools, the students working in small groups are able to converse and discuss.

The meetings are structured and have a set theme for the discussion. The students prepare for these scheduled meetings, working on the vocabulary they will use and preparing simple scripts. The conversations quickly move beyond the scripts and this challenges their comprehension, forcing them to extend and develop it. The class reciprocates with the distant class in English, assisting them to develop their second language skills.

Students can also use FaceTime for these conversations (figure 7.14). However, this application lacks the instant messaging component that allows the students to converse in written language as well as orally.

Figure 7.14—A look at FaceTime

In the paid version of Skype, the class is able to use multiperson video conferencing, allowing for a number of individuals or groups to video conference with each other.

Summary

Learning a language is a multi-faceted affair. The students must understand not only the spoken and written word, but also the culture and, to an extent, the history of the land that has shaped the dialect. All three aspects of language acquisition are interlinked and the tools selected here link culture, spoken, and written language together. Most of the tools allow the students to create and develop their own products, bringing ownership of the learning process to the students. The tools also enable students to converse either across the room or across the world. This in turn supports the understanding of cultures and helps to remove the barriers and obstacles we so often encounter.

Tools for Speaking in Tongues: Apps in the Spotlight

Name: Comic Life

Cost: $4.99

iTunes URL: http://bit.ly/MC6g95

Type: Comic creation tool

Device: iPad

Description: Comic Life is a straightforward and powerful tool for the development of single- or multipage comics. It comes with a number of templates and allows users to develop their own layout and format. The range of layouts available covers most of the different style of comics from the 60s onward, as well as euro comic, futuristic graphical novels, and manga. A comic is unlimited in the number of pages, and navigation between pages is by a sideways one-finger flick. The user can add and manipulate image place holders, increasing and decreasing size, rotating, and moving. Students are able to add a number of speech and thought bubbles, as well as callout boxes and shapes. Images can be added either directly from the camera or from the photo library and camera roll. Comics can be shared via email as images or PDF files, through social networks, and printed via connected printers.

Name: Google Earth

Cost: Free

iTunes URL: http://bit.ly/OMRuPq

Type: Basic geographical information system and mapping tool

Device: iPad / iPod Touch / iPhone

Description: Google Earth is a free application that links to the Google Earth servers. The product allows the user to view different locations around the world. Different layers or overlays can be switched on or off showing places, businesses, panoramic photos, roads, borders, and labels. Sliding two fingers up and down the image will change the viewing angle from overhead to nearly horizontal and back again. Double-tapping with a single finger will zoom in and double-tapping with two fingers will zoom out. The application links to Wikipedia, allowing students to quickly access pertinent information about the locations they are investigating.

Name: iTranslate

Cost: Free

iTunes URL: http://bit.ly/N6ROXN

Type: Online translation tool

Device: iPad / iPod Touch / iPhone

Description: iTranslate is a multiple language translation tool. Phrases are entered in one language, and then translated into a wide selection of other languages, including Spanish, French, German, Italian, Japanese, and more. With some languages, you are able to play back the oral translation as well as see the written translation. In the subscription version, spoken phrases are translated. Students are also able to create lists of terms and phrases and save them.

Name: Play2Learn French

Cost: $1.99

iTunes URL: http://bit.ly/RfPtxZ

Type: Oral/written vocabulary development in a range of languages

Device: iPad

Description: This is a graphical oral language vocabulary tool. Students click on a themed palette to select it, and then can learn the vocabulary by repetition and test themselves in the testing mode. The written form of the word is available by hovering over the cartoon-style image. This application is available in a wide range of languages suiting the ESL or foriegn language learner. The application has a number of extensions that contain more themes. The language packs will cover many of the basic nouns required for day-to-day activities and conversation. Extension packs are available for purchase through the application.

Name: Skype

Cost: Basic version is free; paid version allows a wider feature set including multiparty video conferencing

iTunes URL: http://bit.ly/OL0LcD

Type: Audio and video conferencing tool with instant messaging

Device: iPad / iPod Touch / iPhone

Description: Skype is a free download that allows you to audio and video conference with a single recipient or audio conference with multiple recipients. The basic version requires the user to register the product using an email address. Users then select an online name and set their personal privacy settings to suit their needs. Files can be transfered using instant messaging. Skype also allows the user to send short messages during the audio conference or without audio or video conferencing.

Name: SpellBoard

Cost: $4.99

iTunes URL: http://bit.ly/PqySkM

Type: Spelling testing and reinforcement tool

Device: iPad

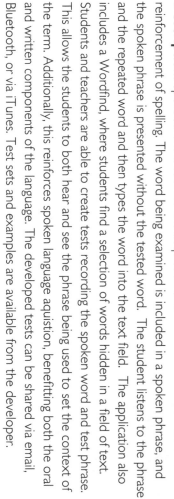

Description: SpellBoard is a tool for the acquisition and reinforcement of spelling. The word being examined is included in a spoken phrase, and the spoken phrase is presented without the tested word. The student listens to the phrase and the repeated word and then types the word into the text field. The application also includes a Wordfind, where students find a selection of words hidden in a field of text. Students and teachers are able to create tests recording the spoken word and test phrase. This allows the students to both hear and see the phrase being used to set the context of the term. Additionally, this reinforces spoken language aquistion, benefitting both the oral and written components of the language. The developed tests can be shared via email, Bluetooth, or via iTunes. Test sets and examples are available from the developer.

Chapter 8

Tools for
**Sharing and
Talking**

8 Tools for Sharing and Talking

Collaboration or sharing is part of 21st-century learning. When students work on projects together they are not only collaborating with their peers in the classroom, but also with students in different parts of the world. Using online storage is becoming the norm that gives students access to their files at any time on any computer.

The following apps are used for sharing and are quickly moving from the business world to the classroom. With the shift to mobile devices, teachers can have a shared homework folder as well as a homework collection folder. Videos can be posted through the apps or embedded to websites, and students can add comments as part of their assessments. These files can be viewed at any time, and students can watch videos and view images or documents both inside and outside the classroom with Internet connectivity.

Teachers can create videos on their interactive whiteboards and make them available to students as part of the "Homework Helpline" or flipped classroom. These are online storage apps that are free for personal use. If you need more storage, there are charges for additional online space. There are also "school locker" programs available to schools.

Dropbox

This service provides free online storage for your data—up to 2GB initially. You can access your Dropbox from anyplace there is Internet connectivity, including a desktop, laptop, tablet, phone, and so on. Dropbox is ideal for online storage in a 1:1 environment because when you log in you stay logged in until you log out.

Dropbox is a preferred online storage app for many other apps. One of these is Quickoffice Pro HD, an app for creating, editing, and sharing Microsoft Office files. This app uses Dropbox and several other applications for online storage so that users can access, transfer, and manage their files (figure 8.1).

Figure 8.1—Available applications in Quickoffice Pro HD

No Flash Drives Needed

Students don't have to carry flash drives with their presentations or other homework assignments on them. They can log in to Dropbox from a classroom computer or iPad/iPod Touch/iPhone and download their files or simply present from the app through a projector attached to the iPad 2 or iPhone 4S.

Jordan, a middle school student, can upload any documents from Quickoffice HD or videos created in Puppet Pals HD that have been saved to the camera roll on the iPad/iPod Touch/iPhone. The example to the left is a map of South America uploaded to Dropbox (figure 8.2).

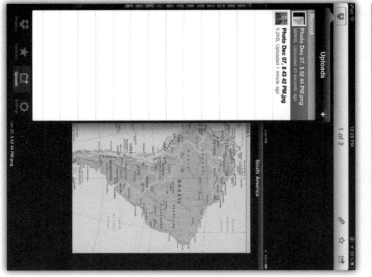

Figure 8.2—Map of South America in Dropbox

Dropbox Folder in My Documents

Jordan often creates documents and videos on his laptop, iPad, and iPod Touch and has Dropbox installed on the computer. Inside his documents folder there is a Dropbox folder where he can easily save to his Dropbox online storage (figure 8.3).

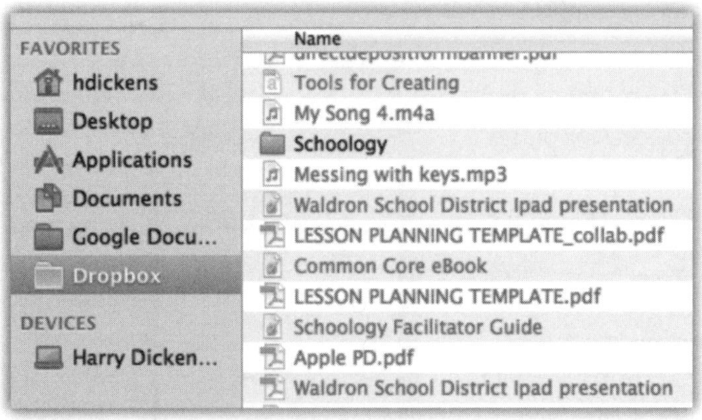

Figure 8.3—Accessing the Dropbox folder

Since he has Dropbox downloaded on all his personal mobile devices, he can be assured that the most current version of any file is available. He doesn't worry about updating or moving files from one machine to another because the files are automatically synced up between devices. To collaborate using Dropbox, Jordan can share documents, images, audio files, videos, and more from his Dropbox. He can also email others a shortened URL automatically created by the application.

As an example, the link created by Dropbox for the image below would be shortened to *http://db.tt/pIuIMX4H*. If you were to click on it, you would be taken to the PDF document below (figure 8.4).

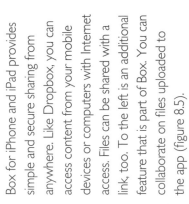
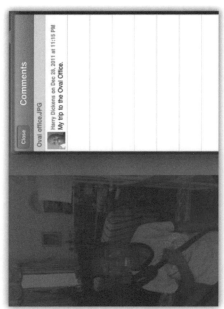

Figure 8.4—Emailing a link from Dropbox is this easy

Box Commenting Tool

Box for iPhone and iPad provides simple and secure sharing from anywhere. Like Dropbox, you can access content from your mobile devices or computers with Internet access. Files can be shared with a link, too. To the left is an additional feature that is part of Box. You can collaborate on files uploaded to the app (figure 8.5).

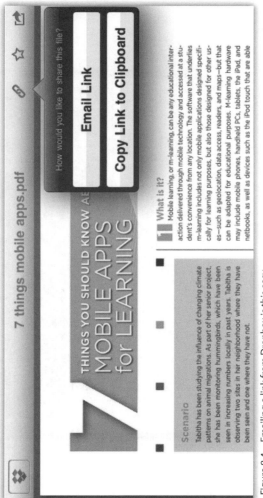

Figure 8.5—Sharing a link in Box

Figure 8.6—Adding a comment in Box

Collaborators can view, edit, and upload files from a computer. Comments can be posted and discussions can be created around files uploaded and opened in Box on the iPad, iPod Touch, iPhone, or computer (figure 8.6).

Box also lets the owner of the documents see what has been downloaded or added to the Box account. Folders in the app can be selected as a favorite folder for offline viewing (figure 8.7). Once added as a favorite, the folder or file becomes available for offline viewing.

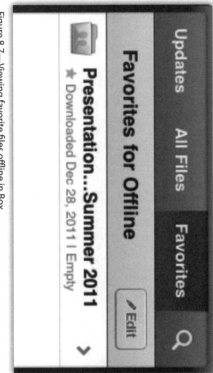

Figure 8.7—Viewing favorite files offline in Box

Uploading Video to Box

With the iPad 2, iPod Touch, or iPhone, users can upload video or images from the camera roll, or videos and pictures can be taken by the device through the app (figure 8.8). This is a must-have when students are collecting videos of experiments or video interviews, or finding angles for a math class and creating a video on how to solve real-world and mathematical problems.

Solving a simple division word problem and having students create a video to keep in Box to share could lead to more challenging problems. Students are hooked by creating the video to show their creative side. An example of a good division word problem might be something like this:

Joey has 28 marbles. He puts them into 4 bags.

He puts the same number of marbles in each bag.

How many marbles are in each bag?

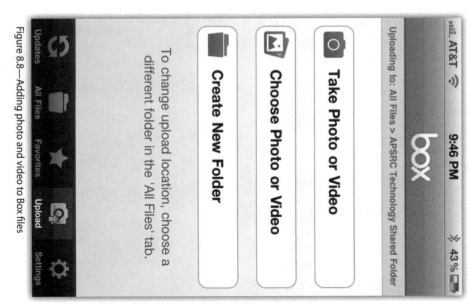

Figure 8.8—Adding photo and video to Box files

To change upload location, choose a different folder in the 'All Files' tab.

Collaboration Through Box

After logging into a Box account, users can add collaborators to folders (figure 8.9). In the technology shared folder below, you will see the two sharing options to folders in Box. One is a secure link to the folder and the other allows you to send an email with a link in the subject line that collaborators can click on to get to the shared folder. Collaborators can then update or share files to this folder.

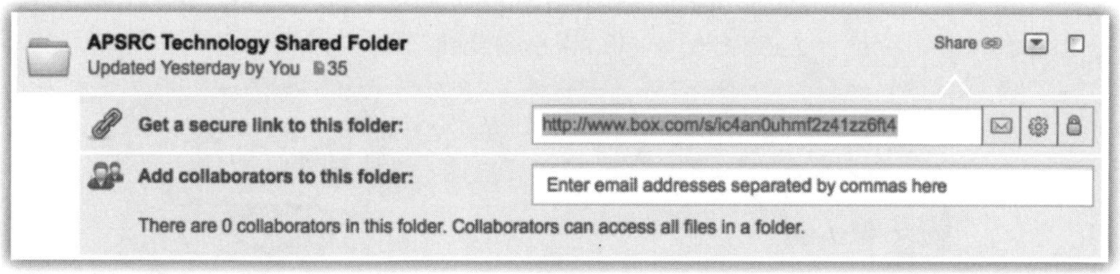

Figure 8.9—Adding collaborators in Box

Files can be sent for preview and download capabilities can be turned off. With the paid version of Box, users can set up mini-accounts within their main account, and then provide a username and password to just that folder, which means no email logins are needed for people under the creator's Box account umbrella. This is a way teachers could provide files to students without email accounts.

Teachers could set up a folder in their account called Students with a common username and password and allow downloading from a device with Internet access, along with the web link to download files from anywhere. These folders can be unshared at anytime.

iCloud/iOS 5

With the update to iOS 5, iPad, iPod Touch, and iPhone users received a feature called iCloud. iCloud can be used on their phone or tablet and their computers. iCloud stores your music, photos, apps, contacts, calendars, and more, and wirelessly pushes them to your iOS 5 devices and computers (figure 8.10).

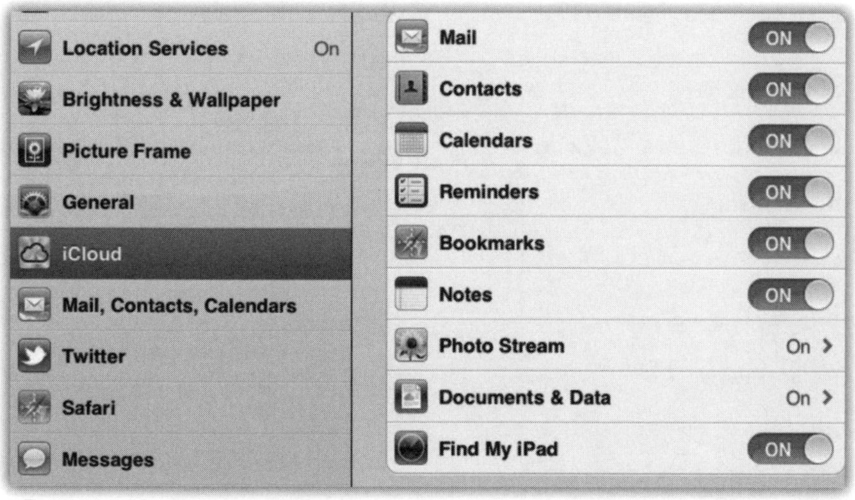

Figure 8.10—Settings menu in iCloud

Syncing over Wi-Fi

A feature educators will appreciate is iCloud's integration with your apps so that everything happens automatically. This makes adding apps to several devices with the same user ID a much quicker process. Apps and books that are purchased appear on iOS devices automatically (figure 8.11). Past purchases of apps and books can be downloaded. Podcasts created on a computer and added to an iTunes playlist can be synced to all devices with the same user account. Student- or teacher-created ebooks or PDF documents can also easily be shared through iTunes and added to the iBook bookshelf.

Automatic Downloads

Music   ON

Apps   ON

Books   ON

Automatically download new purchases (including free) made on other devices.

Figure 8.11—Setting iCloud for automatic downloads

Photo Streaming

Photos taken on any of the devices logged in with the same iTunes account will be sent to all of those devices. If you have a classroom website and a camera at school, then chances are you've looked for a quick and easy way to get your photos on the class web site. Maybe you just took a photo of a blackboard or flipchart lesson or a snapshot of a science experiment and you want to post it online for your students to study. Maybe it's a pic of your school play so that you can celebrate your students' successes. Whatever the case, iCloud may be just the program you need (figure 8.12).

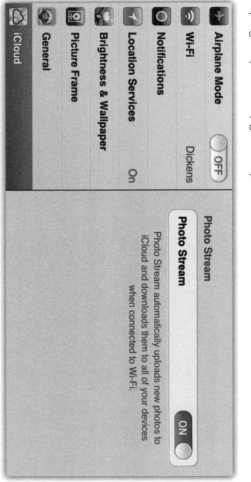

Airplane Mode   OFF

Wi-Fi   Dickens

Notifications

Location Services   On

Brightness & Wallpaper

Picture Frame

General

iCloud

Photo Stream

Photo Stream   ON

Photo Stream automatically uploads new photos to iCloud and downloads them to all of your devices when connected to Wi-Fi.

Figure 8.12—Sending photos to all your devices through iCloud

What Can iCloud Do for Me?

The easier it is to get your photos onto your computer, the easier it is to get those photos to other places like the printer, photo lab, or your web site. Chances are if you took some photos at school, you had to connect your camera or phone to your computer, transfer the photos over, and then upload the photos to your website. If you didn't have your connection cable at school then you had to wait until you got home, and hopefully you didn't get distracted somewhere in between. Take the picture with an iPad 2, 4th generation iPod, or iPhone, and the syncing begins (figure 8.13).

Figure 8.13—Syncing iClod with iPad

Storage Backup and Find My iPad/iPod Touch/iPhone/Mac

iCloud automatically backs up your iOS device daily over Wi-Fi when it's connected to a power source and the device is screenlocked. iCloud backs up your purchased music and TV shows, apps, books, notes, camera roll, device settings, app data, home screen and app organization, messages (iMessage, SMS, and MMS), and ringtones. These backups can be made to iCloud or to the computer. With iCloud, users have 5GB of storage.

If you misplace your iPhone, iPad, iPod Touch, or Mac, you can use Find My iPhone to help you find its location on a map, play a sound at full volume, send a message, lock the screen, or erase its data. You can use the Find My iPhone web application at www.icloud.com on any computer, or download and use the free app on your iOS device (figure 8.14).

Figure 8.14—Finding devices is simple in the settings menu

ShowMe Interactive

ShowMe is an open learning community where you can teach or learn about almost any subject. Watch great lessons for free or create your own with the iPad app. The app is a personal and free interactive whiteboard that both students and teachers can access. Using the ShowMe app with a projector and an Apple TV is a great way to make the class really interactive, with students sharing what is on their screens to the rest of the class. By putting ShowMe into students' hands, we can use learning by teaching to help students truly master a topic, not just prep for it.

Both solution and media fluency are incorporated when using the ShowMe app. Students can define a problem using the whiteboard. They can envision the problem being solved. Then they can deliver the answer and create a digital product to share. Through the application of math problems, middle grade students can see the steps of any problem in motion and truly practice what they need at any time. Students could bring the life cycle of a butterfly to life in science class. ShowMe also allows you to record voiceover whiteboard tutorials and share them online. These videos can be made either public or private.

ShowMe in Algebra

The ShowMe app gives students the opportunity to do a little whiteboard screencasting on the iPad, and it's pretty amazing. Take a snapshot of an equation on a sheet of paper. Then from your camera roll, open the picture in Adobe Photoshop Express and crop the questions you want. When you're done, simply import the picture into ShowMe (figure 8.15).

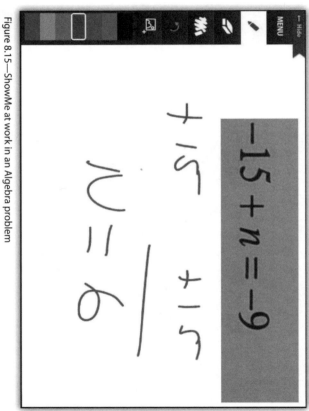

Figure 8.15—ShowMe at work in an Algebra problem

Become Good Tutorial Designers

ShowMe allows you to record voiceover whiteboard tutorials and share them online. It's a radically intuitive app that anyone will find extremely easy to use, regardless of age or background.

Easily switch between drawing and erasing (as well as pausing and playing) to make your ShowMe flow from concept to concept. When it is time to share the work you have done, the window below will appear and you can give the file a name or start over (figure 8.16).

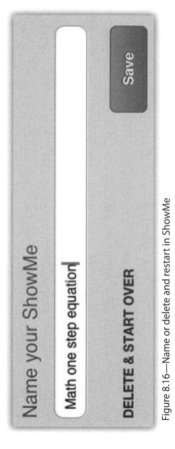

Figure 8.16—Name or delete and restart in ShowMe

Once you're finished recording, upload your ShowMe to share with the community (or keep it private if you prefer (figures 8.17 and 8.18).

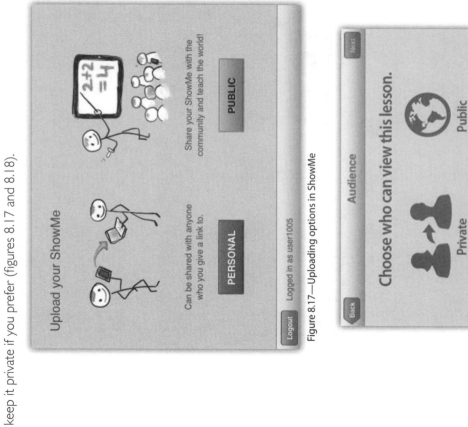

Figure 8.17—Uploading options in ShowMe

Figure 8.18—Share your file or make it private

In the ShowMe Community, you will find hundreds of examples in several content areas. Teachers can add their ShowMe example to their own do-it-yourself blog. An athletic coach could diagram plays and send the plays to the students by posting them to a blog or sending them as an email attachment. ShowMe is an excellent example of a tool to use for flipping your classroom. Now students can watch steps for solutions to problems on the bus or at home. Creating videos for the flipped classroom allows time for lab or interactive activities to illustrate concepts. Uploading to ShowMe is free, and lessons can be of any length.

The file can be sent as an email or as a hyperlink that can be placed on a website or embedded in a learning management system—or wherever else teachers share information with students. This keeps student frustration down, since they have videos that can help them complete homework assignments anywhere at anytime.

Educreations Interactive Whiteboard

Using this app will turn your iPad into an interactive whiteboard and allow you to plan, create, and share lessons in far less time than before. With this amazing app, the act of recording a video lesson and posting it to the Web is significantly easier and less time consuming for teachers and allows educators to create beautiful plans in less time with a product that is fast, fun, and easy to use.

Educreations gives students and teachers the ability to move objects around the screen, such as placing decimals from largest to smallest or creating plays for the basketball court (figure 8.19).

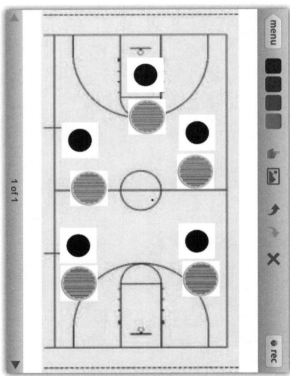

Figure 8.19—Making plays in Educreations

Images can be imported from the camera roll on any mobile device or from Dropbox. In the image on the following page, middle school students can add descriptive words for an image that they normally wouldn't use, alongside descriptive words they would use. This makes their writing more visual than it would be if they were reading something with just text (figure 8.20).

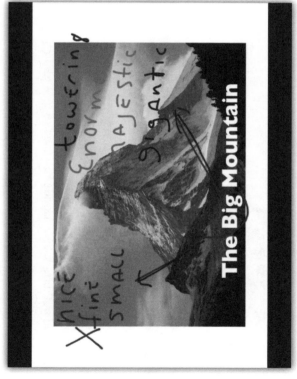

Figure 8.20—Adding writing to a photo in Educreations

The features of this app are highly intuitive to use and make lessons look great. Lessons can also be enhanced by using the iPad features to add pictures from the iPad photo library or a Dropbox account or by snapping photos with the iPad's camera.

All lessons are hosted on www.educreations.com, where teachers can choose to share them privately with their own students or publicly so anyone can view them. Lessons can also be embedded on a blog and shared via Facebook or Twitter (figure 8.21). How amazing is that? You can put your lessons anywhere using this app.

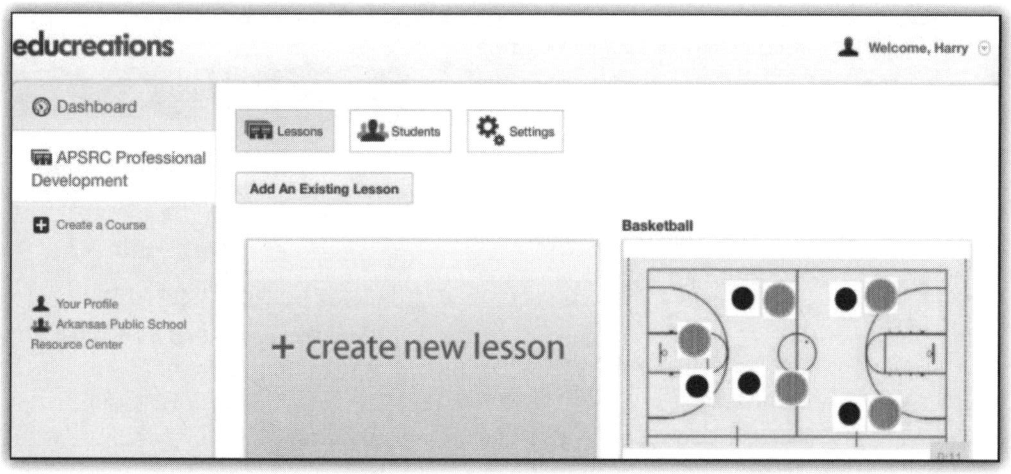

Figure 8.21—Educreations gives you full control over your lessons

There are quite a few features that separate this app from its competitors, including the ability to create multipage lessons and integrate Dropbox. The technology to perform key functions like undo, redo, move, resize, and rotate—all while recording—are enhanced features that replicate working with common office software. Teachers are also able to add individual features such as a student roster, specific logins, and Q and A sessions hosted via Educreations.

Whiteboard HD

The Whiteboard HD app, with its ability to import images from the photo library or Dropbox and Box apps, allows for endless visual possibilities. Charts, images of angles, maps, and more can be annotated. The app also offers flexible and precise drawing tools. It supports freehand drawing, but it also gives you the ability to manipulate text and standard flowchart-type objects with the iPad's multitouch interface (figure 8.22).

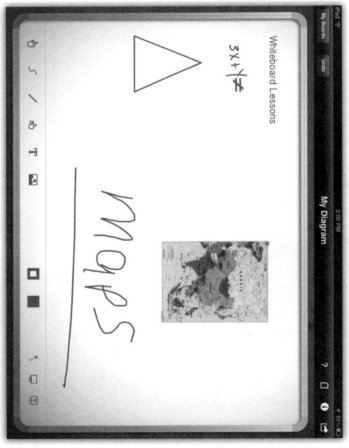

Figure 8.22—Manipulating a map in Whiteboard HD

Teachers can use the integrated laser pointer to add emphasis to what they are explaining. After lessons are completed, the whiteboard activity can be emailed or uploaded to Dropbox, Box, or the iPad's photo library.

The whiteboard screen can also be shared to another device with the app (figure 8.23). Only the owner can manipulate the board during a sharing session. After the sharing is complete, both boards will have that activity.

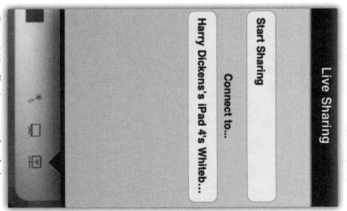

Figure 8.23—Sharing to another device

In geography class, students can develop an understanding of the physical and spatial characteristics and applications of geography. This can be done by importing maps that help them identify and describe the region their state is located in or the locations of major bodies of water and other geographic landmarks (figure 8.24).

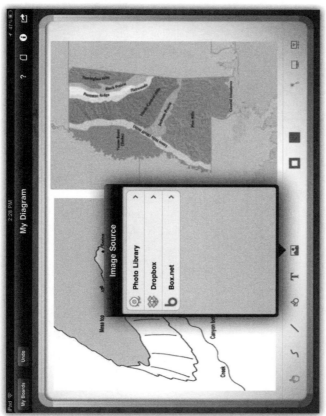

Figure 8.24—Geography with Whiteboard HD

Students can create Venn diagrams to compare the contributions of people of various backgrounds in the development of early civilizations. Teachers or students could make a visual aid to compare and contrast the three branches of government at the state and national levels (figure 8.25).

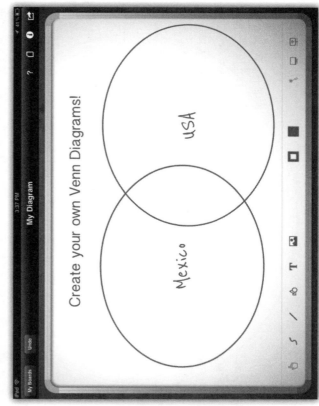

Figure 8.25—A Venn diagram in Whiteboard HD

In a science class, students can use the app to interpret scientific data by creating circle graphs, line graphs, stem and leaf plots, and Venn diagrams very easily with the data they may be working with.

Other possibilities with the app are using it in a physical science lesson. After an initial observation, a student can describe and illustrate plant and animal tissue or illustrate the hierarchical relationships of cells, tissues, organs, and organ systems. In math class, students could use the app to illustrate how to label external and internal angles with the assistance of the triangle and polygon shapes that are a part of the app (figure 8.26).

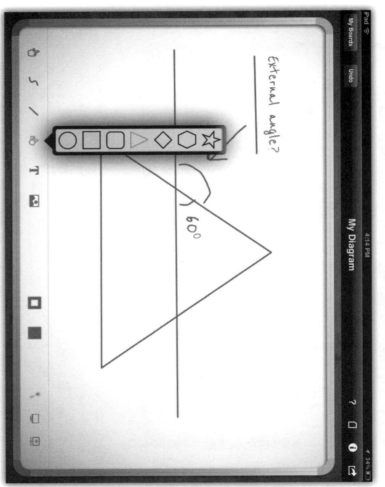

Figure 8.26—Using Whiteboard's geometric shapes in math class

Why Are Whiteboard Apps Important?

Whiteboard HD is a presentation tool that allows any standard that has content to be presented or reviewed on a whiteboard. Students and teachers can present claims and findings, sequencing ideas logically using pertinent descriptions, facts, and details to accentuate main ideas or themes, and use adequate volume and clear pronunciation.

This is a great way to include multimedia components (i.e., graphics, images, music, sound) and/or visual displays in presentations to clarify information. Using the Whiteboard HD app allows for the use of technology to present the relationships between information and ideas efficiently, as well as the ability to interact and collaborate with others.

Splashtop Remote Desktop for iPad and Splashtop Whiteboard

The Splashtop Remote desktop app allows the user to control programs running on a PC or Mac computer. This works over Wi-Fi or 3G/4G network with streaming software loaded onto the computer. After starting the app, the iPad will find computers with the server application on the local network (figure 8.27). A password is required to connect to a computer.

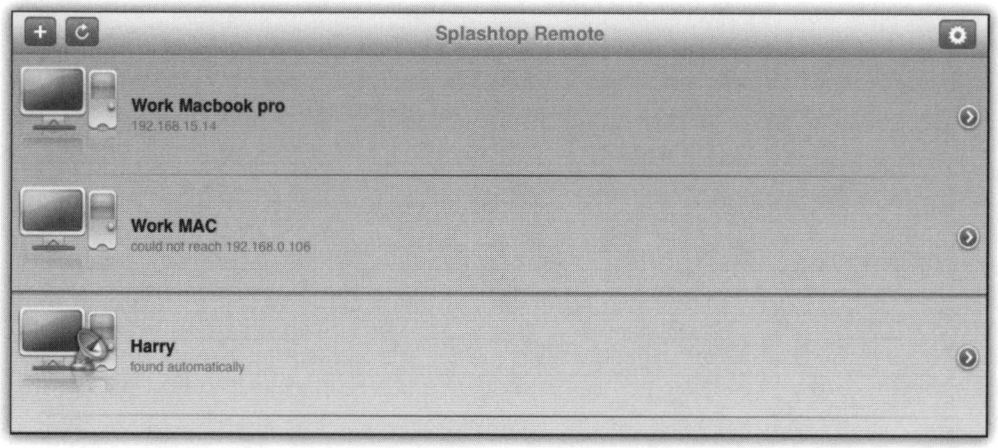

Splashtop Remote
Work Macbook pro
192.168.15.14
Work MAC
could not reach 192.168.0.106
Harry
found automatically
Figure 8.27—Splashtop Remote conveniently finds and lists all computers on your network

Once connected, the iPad can manipulate programs on the computer. The Hints screen is the first screen you will see. It shows the gestures to use on the iPad's screen (figure 8.28).

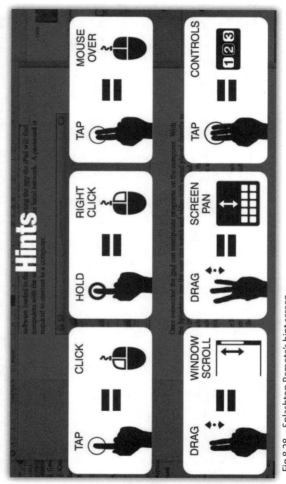

Hints
TAP
CLICK
HOLD
RIGHT CLICK
TAP
MOUSE OVER
DRAG
WINDOW SCROLL
DRAG
SCREEN PAN
TAP
CONTROLS
123
Fig 8.28—Splashtop Remote's hint screen

With the Splashtop app, the user can watch videos with sound played directly to the iPad. Watching flash videos can be viewed by the iPad as well. If teachers want to connect remotely to their desktop from their iPad, they would log in to their gmail account on the server software as well as the iPad application.

The Splashtop Remote Desktop app does not have any tools for drawing, writing, or any other interactive activities, but if interactive whiteboard software is loaded on the computer, it can be controlled from the iPad.

The Splashtop Whiteboard app includes whiteboard tools similar to what we find in most interactive whiteboard software (figure 8.29). Flipcharts can be created and there are several backgrounds to choose from, including KWL charts and graph papers. There is a screen shade for hiding the answer to questions and a spotlight for showing only what you want the class to see.

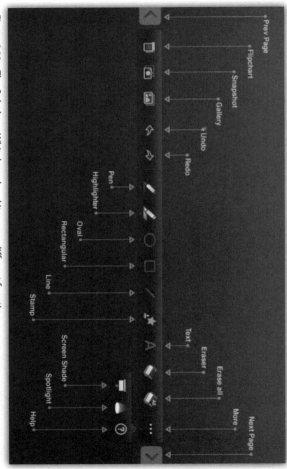

Figure 8.29—The Splashtop Whiteboard and its many different functions

Tools for Sharing and Talking: Apps in the Spotlight

Name: Box.net

Cost: Free

iTunes URL: http://bit.ly/N6U0OU

Type: Business

Device: iPad / iPod Touch / iPhone

Description: Users can view files directly on their iPad/iPod Touch/iPhone. Files can be shared easily with a link. Photos can be uploaded to a Box account with an iPhone. Users can project files from Box to a TV, LCD monitor via a projector with VGA adapters, or using AirPlay (iPad2 and iPhone 4 only). Printing can be done with AirPrint-enabled printers.

Name: Dropbox

Cost: Free

iTunes URL: http://bit.ly/OMS7so

Type: Productivity

Device: iPad / iPod Touch / iPhone

Description: Dropbox is 2GB of online storage that allows for sharing and saving files. The app allows users access from mobile devices, your personal computer with Dropbox loaded onto it, or via the Internet from any computer.

Name: Educreations Interactive Whiteboard

Cost: Free

iTunes URL: http://bit.ly/NpCWRR

Type: Education

Device: iPad

Description: Educreations turns the iPad into a personal interactive whiteboard. Along with voiceover, multiple pages can be added to presentations. After setting up an Educreations account, teachers have options to share to their entire school building or to only their students, or they can keep the creations private.

Name: ShowMe Interactive Whiteboard

Cost: Free

iTunes URL: http://bit.ly/MC8ci7

Type: Education

Device: iPad

Description: The ShowMe Interactive Whiteboard app turns the iPad into a personal interactive whiteboard. ShowMe allows you to add voiceover on whiteboard tutorials and share them online on the ShowMe site or through Facebook, Twitter, or email.

Name: Splashtop 2

Cost: $2.99

iTunes URL: http://bit.ly/NdYe5T

Type: Business

Device: iPad

Description: The only remote app that allows audio and video streaming from the PC or Mac to the iPad. You will also have the ability to stream from any network over Wi-Fi or 3G/4G networks.

Name: Splashtop Whiteboard

Cost: $19.99

iTunes URL: http://bit.ly/OtZe6L

Type: Education

Device: iPad

Description: Splashtop Whiteboard allows teachers and students to turn an iPad into an interactive whiteboard. Once connected to a computer over Wi-Fi, they can watch Flash media with fully synchronized video and audio, control PC and Mac applications, and then annotate lesson content all from an iPad. Now teachers can interact with students at their desks or teach from all four corners of the class!

Name: Whiteboard HD

Cost: $4.99

iTunes URL: http://bit.ly/QyTvCk

Type: Productivity

Device: iPad

Description: Whiteboard HD makes creating visual sketches, note taking, and brainstorming easy and fun. The app allows users to create freeform projects using different shapes and lines. The Whiteboard HD app also allows for videos to be presented using the iPad and iPad 2.

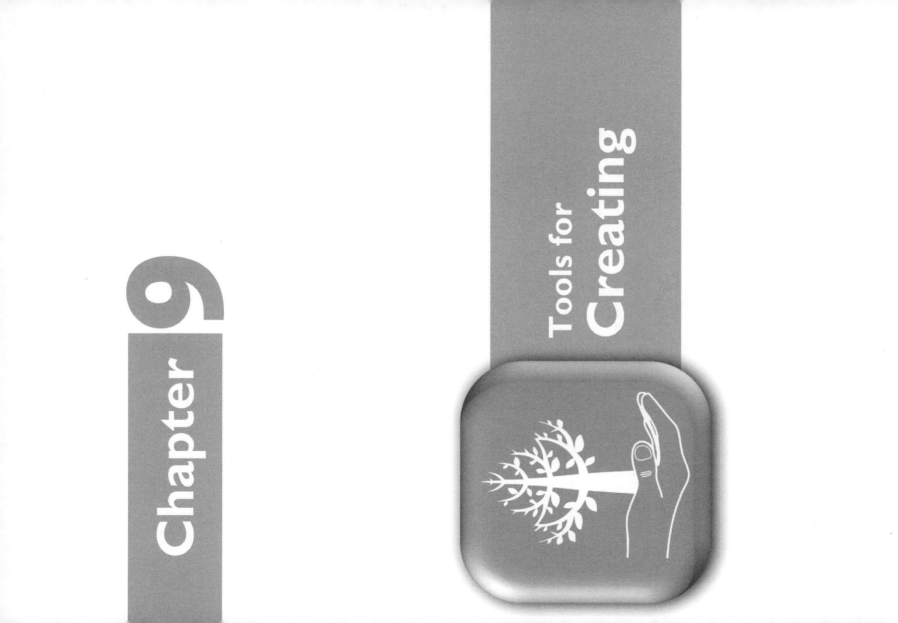

Chapter 9

Tools for Creating

9 Tools for Creating

The education community is a rather creative one, so you would think that creative outbursts such as these would be the norm, and that they would inspire schools and districts to provide these kinds of engaging tools for their teachers and students. The apps on the iPad, iPod Touch, and iPhone allow students and teachers to work with their fingers. Student-created music can be added to the background of a presentation using GarageBand. iMovie can be used to provide a visual account of field trips. Students can create graphic novels with the Comic Life app. The Strip Designer app can be used to explain a procedure in science class, a character analysis in an English classroom, and steps to citizenship in a civics class. PuppetPals HD can be used to personify animals or inanimate objects. The Common Core State Standards allow for the integration of new ideas and technology. The art, music, and drama apps below should add excitement to text-only assignments.

Illustrated Stories

Illustrated stories are a powerful form of popular expression. Formats such as the single cartoon, panel strip, comic book, graphic novel, and illustrated book have been widely used in our culture to communicate and express ideas in dramatic ways (figures 9.1 and 9.2). Comic Life allows a student to start with a blank page to create and design his or her own comic pages. There are several templates with backgrounds already chosen. Comics can help with building complex reading skills.

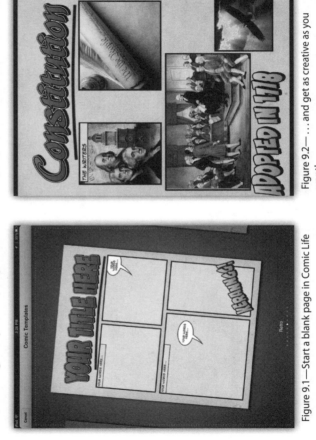

Figure 9.1—Start a blank page in Comic Life

Figure 9.2—…and get as creative as you want!

For example, comics and graphic novels can teach about making interpretations, since readers must rely primarily on pictures and only a small amount of text.

For middle school students, comics can contain all the complexity of normal written material that the student must decode and comprehend, such as puns, alliteration, metaphors, symbolism, point of view, context, inference, and narrative structures. A comic can also be a stepping stone to more complex and traditional written works.

A single pane in a comic can represent paragraphs worth of written material in a manner that is enjoyable and effective for the early or challenged reader. Information fluency can be unconsciously added in comic strips for the visual learner. Students can analyze and arrange materials and turn data into knowledge.

Facilitate Student Participation

Comic Life can breathe new life into an old assignment. Unlike most book reports, visuals can be used to add interest to the document. The book report is a core part of the classroom for several reasons. First, it provides a way to evaluate whether or not a student has read the assigned material. Second, it allows a student to show how he or she synthesizes and analyzes information contained in written material.

Comic Life can help students create and share reports with the class that are fun and interesting. With its paneled interface, Comic Life allows users to break down larger concepts into smaller and more easily digested ideas that can be strung together in a coherent and entertaining way. Creating a project with images can draw a student into the story or into a character in a way that a written report simply can't.

Social Studies/English Language Arts with Comic Life

Harrison is in a middle school social studies class and has a project that requires visuals and a report about famous army generals from World War II (figure 9.3).

Social studies standards require students to understand the contributions of people in the United States as well as other parts of the world. Harrison used Comic Life to create the visuals, and he added most of the text for the assignment inside the cartoon panels.

Another student, James, has a project about the Martin Luther King Jr. memorials in cities around the United States. This is a collaborative project with his partner Sue.

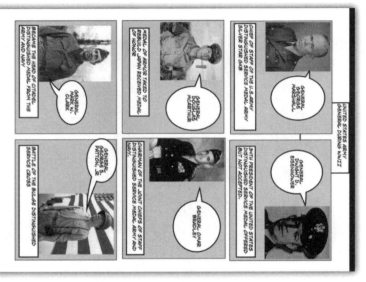

Figure 9.3—WWII generals tell their stories in Comic Life

James has finished the cover page and can place that page in the Comic Life tray for Sue to add to the front of her report (figure 9.4).

Figure 9.4—Learning about Martin Luther King Jr. memorials

Science/English Language Arts with Comic Life

Harrison can use the app in his science class as the class creates reports on pollinators (figure 9.5). The first page is images, and subsequent pages have text and smaller images.

Figure 9.5—Using Comic Life in science class

Similar to the preceding social studies project, this assignment could be created by several students on their iPads, with selected pages shared through the tray of the app. In science class, pollinators could be explored and made into a visual project with the students collaborating and creating their own parts. Including this assignment in the English language arts classroom as a cross-curricular activity, the text for each of the pages can be included on a second page of the Comic Life strip with a one-pane page (figure 9.6).

There are well over 200,000 animal pollinators in the world, with most of them being insects. Jon, Susan, and Scott are middle school students at McRae Middle School. Their project could be to describe three insect pollinators: Honeybees, bumblebees, and butterflies. Since these

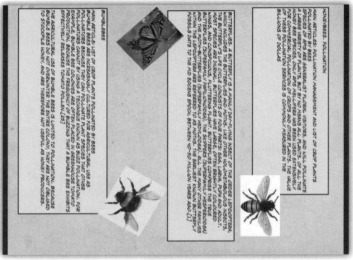

Figure 9.6—Using full text panes in Comic Life

pollinators only pollinate certain plants, images of these plants and the insects could be included in each pane.

Using Comic Life in Math

What does a car really cost? Using this app for visuals, students can break down real-world math problems. In this example, students can choose the vehicle of their choice, go to a car dealership to look at the sticker cost, and take pictures to add to their project. They can also research interest rates and take a snap shot of a billboard of a bank's advertisement on vehicle financing information for their car cost calculations (figure 9.7). The teacher can have set costs for the students to add to their project such as taxes, state charge for the purchase, and registration fees. In this example, students are applying another part of the information fluency process—they are applying knowledge of things they know to a real-world math problem.

Figure 9.7—Showing how much a car "really" costs in Comic Life

The Strip Designer app has some features in common with Comic Life. Images can be brought in from the photo library to several templates which are built into the app. Photos can be shared through the application as well as through Flickr, and photo strips can also be saved as PDF files.

United States Citizenship with Strip Designer

Instead of using a linear presentation tool, Strip Designer can be used to have all of the images on one page. If text is needed, students can add a few words through a word cloud to prod their memory if speaking in front of a crowd. In this example, Harrison used the Strip Designer app to make a visual of the patterns of migration to the United States (figure 9.8). In his project, the questions asked were:

- Who are "Americans," and where did they come from?
- How does a person become a U.S. citizen?

Figure 9.8—A citizenship project using Strip Designer

His linear presentation also demonstrates that Harrison used Strip Designer to create and publish with digital media as effectively as he could with text. If he were presenting in front of his peers, he could confidently look at the images and speak about each of the periods and their dates and how people came to the United States.

Working Unit Rate Problems and Including Onomatopoeia with Strip Designer

In this problem, Jordan has a job mowing lawns and has forty hours this summer for this task. Jordan makes $400. He's excited, but this can be a real-world problem for him as well as other students. Students who are interested in working in sales need to understand that they have to sell whatever the product is to make money. This scenario is a great example of turning a math problem into storytelling (figure 9.9). Jordan is learning about units and rate as well as creating onomatopoeia for his literacy classroom. His creativity fluency skills are shown with the image of the clock to make his visual about time, and the lawn mower to visualize his lawn mowing job. This problem could be solved with images of a babysitting job or even chores around the house.

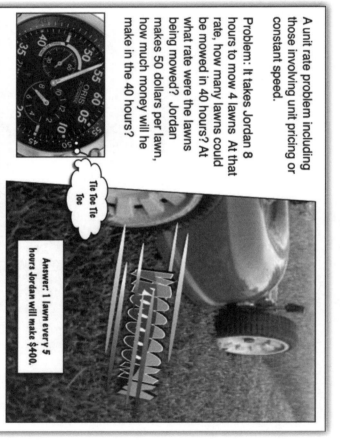

A unit rate problem including those involving unit pricing or constant speed.

Problem: It takes Jordan 8 hours to mow 4 lawns At that rate, how many lawns could be mowed in 40 hours? At what rate were the lawns being mowed? Jordan makes 50 dollars per lawn, how much money will he make in the 40 hours?

Tic Toc Tic Toc

Answer: 1 lawn every 5 hours Jordan will make $400.

Figure 9.9—Storytelling and math come together in Strip Designer

What Happened? (Illustration Apps)

When looking at the illustrations from the preceding applications, you will see examples of trying to make the images do most of the talking. Students will use more than simple remembering skills working with these apps. They'll get to apply their artistic skills to create something visual that shows what they know. Before giving a speech about the founding fathers, a student can create a visual to go with the speech, and some students may be able to recite their speech using the Comic Life pages as their note cards.

Adding images that replicate what you want readers to understand is very important when illustrating. How many middle school students know there may be a bank involved when purchasing a car? Their next question should be: "How do banks make money?" The interest they charge for borrowing money is one way. The Strip Designer illustration on migration to the United States is a great visual that will not need many word to describe the different blocks of history.

Puppet Pals HD

Storytelling

The Puppet Pals HD app allows users to choose characters, backgrounds, and resize images. When you're ready, push the record button, move your characters around, and narrate your story. Within minutes, users can have an animated story. The story can then be shared via email, a web page, a blog, Facebook, and so on. The educational value is limitless (literacy, listening and speaking, drama). Puppet Pals HD with the Director's Pass will allow users to create puppet shows with several characters, including politicians, pirates, farm animals, and even holiday characters from the Christmas and Thanksgiving seasons (figure 9.10).

Figure 9.10—Politics in Puppet Pals HD

There are backgrounds that include the farm, the White House, talk show stages, and more. The Director's Pass allows you to use the camera or photo library on the iPad, iPod Touch, or iPhone to import your own images for characters or backgrounds. The videos created can be exported to the camera roll and even put into iMovie for a video collage of a student's projects.

Trickster Tales and Personifications in Puppet Pals HD

This is an overview for a sample unit found at http://commoncore.org/free/index.php/maps/grade_5_unit_3/. This unit begins with students collectively defining and discussing the word "culture." Next, students compare 19th-century America from the Ojibway point of view in *The Birchbark House*, to depictions in texts such as *Little House on the Prairie* and *If You Were a Pioneer on the Prairie*. In order to glean the similarities and differences across nations, students read trickster stories and informational text, as well as listen to music and examine art from a variety of Native American cultures.

As part of learning about the word "culture" in the English language arts classroom, Jordan can create trickster tales about westward expansion using Puppet Pals HD (figure 9.11).

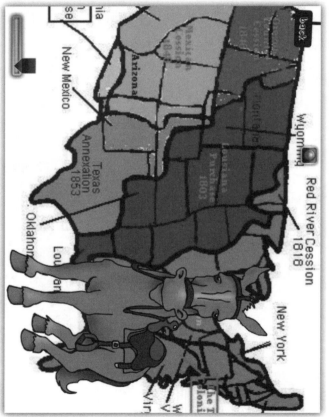

Figure 9.11—Puppet Pals HD brings the westward expansion alive

He can use characters like the horse for personification and use his voice to record what he has learned about westward expansion. There were also conflicts between Native American and European settlers, and images can be used to discuss these conflicts. Jordan and others can collaborate and use images found through Internet searches to show where conflicts happened and record accounts of battles (figure 9.12).

Figure 9.12—Using historical images in Puppet Pals HD

The students can create a visual about the people of the time. They can read about Chief Joseph from the Nez Perc'e to create a Puppet Pals HD visual of what they have read. Of course, there would not have been microphones to do the interview process in figure 9.12, but we want to students ask questions! A creative student is using creativity fluency in the project by using his imagination to get an actual interview with Chief Joseph. The web resource to do this can be found at http://www.pbs.org/weta/thewest/people/a_c/chiefjoseph.htm.

With its backdrop features, Puppet Pals HD could be used to interview famous people from around the world. The students could find images of Winston Churchill, Abraham Lincoln, and others to discuss events that happened during their lifetime (figure 9.13).

Figure 9.13—Interviewing Abraham Lincoln in Puppet Pals HD

GarageBand and iMovie

The GarageBand and iMovie apps can be integrated easily into the literacy and social studies classrooms in middle school. Students can construct book talks and integrate visual information by using images added to iMovie and audio created in GarageBand. Teachers can use GarageBand and iMovie to introduce topics, and these multimedia products will aid comprehension for students. Any GarageBand or iMovie file can be added to an iBook created with iBooks Author on a Mac computer. After being created, they can be shared via email, a web page post, or iTunes. Students can synthesize information into a coherent understanding of a process or concept using these apps. Infusing drama, speech, music, and art into any of the core subjects with these apps is a true example of project-based learning.

iPad / iPod Audio Tours

With GarageBand, students can collaborate in small groups to create an audio tour of an exhibit during a field trip. They can record personal reactions, ambient sounds, and information learned about an exhibit.

They can create audio recordings, and then add their music to the background using GarageBand (figure 9.14).

Figure 9.14—GarageBand's audio recording feature

Adding iMovie to a Project

Jordan has photos from Internet resources of the Little Rock Nine memorial in Little Rock, Arkansas. He can now add his audio project to images. The completed project can be emailed to the teacher or his classmates for critiquing or added to the camera roll, iTunes, YouTube, Vimeo, and other online sites (figure 9.15). The presentation for the field trip can now have authentic sounds and images.

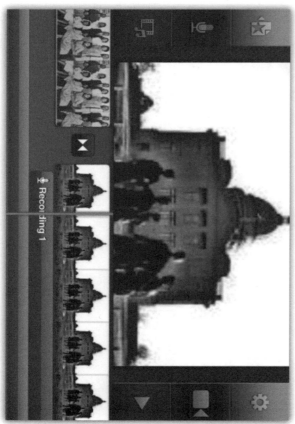

Figure 9.15—iMovie and GarageBand work together perfectly in any project

Children's Theater

Students can use the sound effects, music, and recording features of GarageBand to create a story. The app has a piano keyboard, drums, guitar, microphone, and a guitar amp for creating these sound effects. Students can create an audio book demonstrating an understanding of figurative language. GarageBand can be used to show a student's understanding of synonyms, antonyms, and homographs. So instead of homograph worksheets, images captured by the iPad, iPod Touch, iPhone camera, or from Internet resources can be used to show the different meanings of words (figure 9.16). In this example, the student has to describe a small motorcycle. The sample sentence is: *She moped because her moped is broken.*

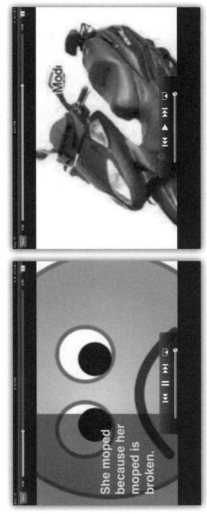

Figure 9.16—Exploring the meanings of different words

Make It a Rap

To support comprehension or fluency, students can use GarageBand to make a rap. Jordan loves creating his own "beats"—he can create a background beat in GarageBand and write a rap of things that have to be memorized in a class, such as scientific principles or mathematical formulas. He is also using fluency in literacy by creating a podcast of prose or poetry to show accuracy, appropriate rate, and expression on successive readings. Jordan and other students can collaborate to create projects, and he can add his rap to a video created in iMovie. Now students can be the creators with iPads in any classroom! They could even use iBooks Author to create a book of their raps with lyrics. What about using it to create karaoke tracks for science principles and mathematical formulas?

Foreign Language Podcast and Video

In his Spanish class, Jordan can use iMovie to translate a short cartoon or movie clip into the studied language and re-record the lines, creating a new version of the movie or TV show for viewing in the new language. Jordan's class also has to discuss historical or current contributions of individuals representing other languages or cultures (e.g., writers, artists, scientists, inventors, mathematicians, political leaders, historical figures, explorers, migrants, immigrants, or athletes). The students can use GarageBand to create a podcast to meet the project requirements or use iMovie if they want to incorporate images or create videos for the assignment.

What Happened? (Storytelling Apps)

Storytelling with these apps brings out students' creativity because they are easy to use and they give artistic students a chance to shine. They can show their talents with sound effects and by setting a tone for the story with the way they speak when adding narration. Several students can be involved in storytelling projects. These projects take on a life of their own with students who become perfectionists when creating something for peers to see and possibly review—a great real-world setting that some have not experienced.

Tools for Creating: Apps in the Spotlight

Name: Comic Life

Cost: $4.99

iTunes URL: http://bit.ly/MC6g95

Type: Photo and video

Device: iPad

Description: Comic Life is the award-winning comic creation software that has been redesigned for the iPad. With Comic Life, you can create photo comics with a full-featured editor. Comics can be shared on Facebook, Twitter, or via email. Comics can be printed to a printer on your wireless network. Comics can be shared with other iPad users on the same network through an innovative tray that is part of the app. Photos from your photo library can easily be placed into the panels in the application. Images, balloons, captions, and lettering can easily be resized and rotated in the apps workspace.

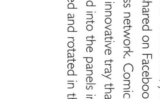

Name: GarageBand

Cost: $4.99

iTunes URL: http://bit.ly/OKSkOi

Type: Music

Device: iPad / iPod Touch / iPhone

Description: GarageBand turns the iPad/iPod Touch/iPhone into a recording studio with touch instruments and audio recording capability. Podcasts can be created for classroom activities by students and teachers. Up to eight tracks can be added to any song or podcast. Files created in GarageBand can also be exported to GarageBand on another device to continue the refining and editing process.

Name: iMovie

Cost: $4.99

iTunes URL: http://bit.ly/OKSkOi

Type: Photo and video

Device: iPad2 / iPod Touch / iPhone

Description: Users can make high-definition movies anywhere with iMovie. iMovie puts everything you need to tell your story at your fingertips. Field trip movies, science project movies, historical figures movies, and more can be created with themes, background music, and sound effects. Movies created with iMovie can be shared right from the app.

Name: Puppet Pals HD

Cost: Free / $2.99 (for the Director's Pass)

iTunes URL: http://bit.ly/Ovdkal

Type: Photo and video

Device: iPad / iPod Touch / iPhone

Description: With Puppet Pals HD, students and teachers can create unique shows with animation and audio in real time! Simply pick out your actors and backdrops, drag them on to the stage, and tap record. Your movements and audio will be recorded in real time for playback later. Interview a head of state or illustrate a culture by choosing characters from those included in the app, or take a photo with your iPad/iPod Touch/iPhone camera or insert images from the camera roll. Create an actor from a photo; use a photo as a backdrop for your storytelling; and zoom and rotate your characters using two fingers, or flip them around with a double tap. This app offers a wide variety of creative characters to download, including famous talk show hosts and politicians, allowing for limitless possibilities of story creations. Additionally, if you buy the Director's Pass for $2.99, you receive all current and future content.

Name: Strip Designer

Cost: $2.99

iTunes URL: http://bit.ly/OESJlm

Type: Photo and video

Device: iPad / iPod Touch / iPhone

Description: With one of the more than one hundred strip templates, students can create graphic comic strips. Text balloons, as well as a selection of more than one hundred stickers, can be used to add pizazz to your comic strip. Maps can be imported as image files from inside Strip Designer, and there is also a drawing whiteboard included in the app.

Apps List

A

Adobe Reader (PDF) 10

Al Gore—Our Choice: A Plan to Solve the Climate Crisis 75

B

Book Creator 26

Box.net 112

C

The Civil War Today 36

Comic Life 88, 99, 132

D

Dictionary 21

Drawing Pad 22

Dropbox 111

E

Educreations Interactive Whiteboard 120

F

FaceTime 103

Field Protractor 57

Frog Dissection 76

G

GarageBand 139

Goodreader 54

Google Earth 95

Grammar Express: Active and Passive Voice 14

Grammar Express: Nouns HD 14

Grammar Express: Parts of Speech 13

Grammar Express: Tenses 14

I

iBooks 1, 23
iCloud 115
iLiveGrammar Autumn 15
iLiveGrammar Botany 15
iLiveGrammar Winter 15
iMovie 51, 139
iPhoto 7
iThoughtsHD 1, 49
iTranslate 84
iWorks (Pages, Keynote, Numbers) 1

J

Japanese Phrases 88

K

Kindle 10
MathBoard 56
Mathletics 56

N

NASA 69

P

Photoshop Express 7
Photoshop Touch 7
Play2Learn English 81
Popplet 10
Prezi 67
Puffin 56
Puppet Pals HD 19, 137

Q

Quickoffice 1

R

Rat Dissection 65
Rover (flash enabled) 1

S

Safari 1

Sentence Builder 83

ShowMe Interactive Whiteboard 118

SimpleMind+ 10

Sketchpad Explorer 54

Skype 103

Sock Puppets 88

Solar Walk 69

SpellBoard 18, 85

SpellBoard Buddy 18

Spelling Test 17

Splashtop Remote Desktop for iPad 125

Splashtop Whiteboard 125

Star Walk 69

StoryKit 19

Strip Designer 135

T

This Day in History 35

U

U.S. Geography by Discovery Education 36

USA Factbook and Quiz 40

V

VoiceThread 67

W

Whiteboard HD 67, 122

Wikihood Plus for iPad 41

World Factbook for iPad 38

Y

Young Reader 27

A whole new way to look at our books.

If you've experienced Al Gore's *Our Choice* or E.O. Wilson's *Life on Earth*, you've seen the future of interactive reading. Now the series of books of the 21st Century Fluency Project is getting an interactive upgrade using iBooks Author for the iPad in 2012.

We're showing you a whole new reading experience using interactive images, video, and all the capabilities offered by Apple's unique digital book creator. It's our books like you've never seen them before, in full vibrant color and literally alive right on your iPad screen.

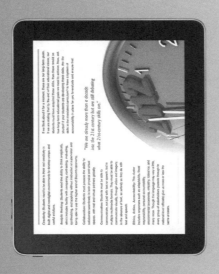

Beginning with *Literacy is Not Enough*, the 21st Century Fluency Series comes into digital format in late 2012. All our iBooks digital versions will be available exclusively for iPad. Get ready to enjoy the new way to experience 21st Century change with our all new iBooks!

Coming soon in 2012!

Get caught up in our Web.

Recent Unit Plans

Imagine a place where you and educators just like you can all share your greatest ideas and visions for 21st-century learning in a supportive and collaborative atmosphere. It's a place where the learning is global and universal—an exciting online educational community that is truly committed to real change in education.

We welcome you to join us in just such a place beginning in 2012!

Recent Activity

This year, the 21st Century Fluency Project is proud to be bringing you the online Fluency Kit Web App. Post your own unique project-based unit plans. Share your ideas with other teachers from all over the world. Add comments and suggestions to innovate and inspire.

The Fluency Kit Web App will allow you to share lesson plans and collaborate with educators across the globe. And there is no better way to make the shift towards bringing new adventures in learning into our 21st Century classrooms.

Visit www.fluency21.com to learn more